"GORDY-ISMS"
BOOK TWO

G.L. EWELL

Engineer Castle

"GORDY-ISMS" BOOK TWO

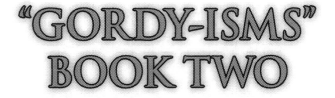

Uplifting and Thought-Provoking Quotes;
Proverbial Dung from the Mountain-top

GORDON L EWELL

Order this book online at www.trafford.com
or email orders@trafford.com

Most Trafford titles are also available at major online book retailers.

© Copyright 2013 Gordon L Ewell.
All rights reserved. No part of this publication may be reproduced, stored in a
retrieval system, or transmitted, in any form or by any means, electronic, mechanical,
photocopying, recording, or otherwise, without the written prior permission of the author.

Printed in the United States of America.

ISBN: 978-1-4907-1967-2 (sc)
ISBN: 978-1-4907-1969-6 (hc)
ISBN: 978-1-4907-1968-9 (e)

Library of Congress Control Number: 2013920931

Because of the dynamic nature of the Internet, any web addresses or links contained in
this book may have changed since publication and may no longer be valid. The views
expressed in this work are solely those of the author and do not necessarily reflect the
views of the publisher, and the publisher hereby disclaims any responsibility for them.

Any people depicted in stock imagery provided by Thinkstock are models,
and such images are being used for illustrative purposes only.
Certain stock imagery © Thinkstock.

Trafford rev. 11/25/2013

www.trafford.com

North America & international
toll-free: 1 888 232 4444 (USA & Canada)
fax: 812 355 4082

For Charlie Wiseacre and everyone who could use a smile and a laugh to start their day.

Carry out random acts of kindness, with no expectation of reward, safe in the knowledge that one day someone might do the same for you.

—Princess Dianna
Princess of Wales

CONTENTS

LIST OF ILLUSTRATIONS

Illustrations are listed in the order in which they appear. First is its name, then it's location within the book

PREFACE

Character is like a tree and reputation like a shadow.
The shadow is what we think of it; the tree is the real thing.
                                                    —Abraham Lincoln

I f I had but a nickel for every time I wished that I could stop
time, or rather go back in time and then stop time, I would be a
millionaire. I was severely injured in the war in Iraq in 2006. As a
career soldier, I was proud of my chosen profession. I was honored
to be a "Defender of Freedom." I was among the very best at what I
did as a soldier. When I was called upon to go to war, of course, I had
some fears. But one thing I knew was that I would return from the
war. I had confidence in my skills and my training, and I knew well
the dangers of my mission and was prepared for it. I knew I would
be successful and come home. I never dreamed I would come home
severely wounded. My mission was in a nutshell, to find the roadside
bombs and ensure other teams, with this dangerous mission, had the
latest intelligence, the skills, and the equipment to be successful.
At that time (2006), there were over 3,100 roadside bombs being
found by our soldiers every month, over a hundred every day. During
that time, a vehicle I was riding in was blown up on six different
occasions. One bomb blast too many left me severely wounded,
and permanently disabled, for the rest of my life; something I never
dreamed would happen! I had a long, painful recovery road to travel;
to get put back together again. Put back together the best that

forty-nine different Health care Specialists, surgeries, stays in six different hospitals in three different states (including a Level One Poly Trauma Ward in Palo Alto, CA) and years of therapy following it all could do anyway. I found myself wanting to stop time prior to getting wounded in combat. I didn't want to have a broken neck, a severe traumatic brain injury, and permanent neurological damage. I did not want to lose an eye, to be legally blind and deaf. I didn't want to need a wheelchair, walker, and canes to get around. I didn't want to never be able to drive a vehicle again, to be homebound, to be in chronic pain, or to suffer daily with post-traumatic stress disorder (PTSD). I didn't want to be on a liquid diet for over four years while getting my face and mouth rebuilt. I wanted to stop time to a period in my past when I was happy, carefree, and in prime physical condition. Eight years now have past, and I realize now that all the years of hurt and pain and a long arduous recovery have forged and strengthened my character far beyond what it could have ever been! Though broken, I have been blessed beyond measure, in ways I could never have been, or even imagined, prior to my combat injuries. I now seek every day to improve upon that: to "be a tree, a very big tree!" I have an appreciation for and depth of understanding for life and love and the fragility of both that I never would have had. I can be happy and very grateful for my life. I now feel humbled, and indeed very blessed.

Just What Is a "Gordy-Ism?"

After being severely wounded during the war in Iraq, there were times during my recovery and rehabilitation when I felt only darkness a lot of pain and agony. More than once, suicide seemed a brighter alternative. Just to make it through a single day was a big victory. I told myself, if I could think of just one positive thought, or thing to be thankful for at the beginning of each day and write it down;

that when the dark images or the pain was getting unbearable, that one positive thought could help fight the images off or help lessen the pain. If I could pull the piece of paper out my pocket that my thought was written on and read it out loud or even just hold the small piece of paper I wrote it on in a closed fist, it would help me get through the darkness. Or at least let enough light in, to help me win a battle and just simply make it through one more day. I would focus on one day at a time, just a day at a time. I would do this every day. It seemed to help. I soon began sharing my daily thoughts with others who were fighting their own battles of recovery, along with me, and with a few people in general that were close to me. They began to look forward to me sharing my little daily thought with them . . .

My first name is Gordon. Everyone calls me "Gordy."

My peers began to refer to my thoughts for the day as "Gordy-isms." It stuck, and so began the birth of "Gordy-isms," and a practice I continue to do. I think of something positive each morning and write it down to start my day.

I now share them in my writings and on the computer with others via the Internet on my websites and Facebook pages.

So, What Are "Gordy-Isms?"

They are short inspirational, uplifting, or thought-provoking little quip-it's, or intended to be anyway—a little thought to start your day with a smile.

I hope you enjoy them! I hope they bring smiles, warm your heart when needed, and perhaps provide a laugh or two when needed as well.

I don't profess to be full of profound wisdom or have some superior depth of intellectual insight into the mind, body, and soul or profess to have the answers to any questions.

I am just a "broken ol' warrior" who tries to get a couple of brain cells to bump into each other in the morning and spark a little thought to start my day off on a good note. I am my own little "Blue Collar Philosopher", if you will.

Thank you for letting me share with you, my "Gordy-isms!"

THE BEST THING TO
HOLD ONTO IN LIFE
IS EACH OTHER.
　　　　-AUDREY HEPBURN

SECTION ONE

Friends and Friendship

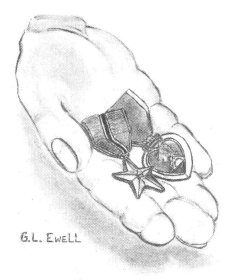

G.L. EWELL

Hand of Honor

Far greater than any medals, titles, or accolades is the knowledge that you have a best friend, and are one to someone else as well.

T he shortest distance to travel between two points is a long walk with a dear friend.

While not being able to "move" the "potholes" in the "road of life" we choose to travel on, good friends have the ability to at least steer us around them.

If a friend is driving you absolutely *crazy*, by constantly reminding you of something that *you* asked them to . . . it is a true friend you should not be upset with, but rather take care of. Because obviously, they truly care about *you!*

No one will ever have a life in which every day is warm, sunny, and full of nothing but fun and laughter. However, that is where good friends and loved ones come in. They are the warm coats wrapped around us, the gloves, and the scarfs; they provide the funny joke to lift our spirits and bring us laughter. Even on those days that feel turbulent and full of storm clouds that are blocking the sun, they are the "rays of sunlight" that break through the "storm clouds" in our lives!

Friends have a special way of letting you know and have confidence that they will always tell you if your "fly" is unzipped, your shoe is untied, you have ice cream on your moustache, or your "fake-eye" is upside down, all before you get embarrassed in public, but not before they get a good laugh! They always laugh "with" you not "at" you, however.

One of the most wonderful things about true friends is their ability to, without passing judgment, be a simple mirror of reflection that allows us to see who we are and see our good qualities and good points (which we all have) when we are feeling down and need a boost of self-confidence and love.

Friends afford us the opportunity to learn life's lessons on our own. Even if we make mistakes, or get hurt, they are there to help pick us up, dust us off, and continue our journey, making us know we are loved and appreciated every step of the way.

Sharing a secret . . . has an old friend been on your mind? Has it been a while since you heard from family or loved ones? I have a secret I'll share that will put their voice in your ear in less than a minute. What's the secret? Quit using your phone as a paper weight, stop waiting for it to ring, and call them! You don't want to be the person that, while mourning, says, "I *wish* I would have called and let them know I loved them . . ."

When faced with adversity, one has but two choices: to square your shoulders to it and throw the punches you need to in order to get through it or turn and run, letting it wear you down, which it will because it will jump onto your back, slow your pace, and always be there until you do decide to face it. Some troubles are too big for one person to handle. For the big monsters just remember, that is why we have been blessed with friends! When it comes to friends, it is not the quantity you have that matters most, but it's the quality.

Good friends are like an umbrella in a downpour, as they are always there to keep the storms of life from drenching you.

Life is full of "ups and downs" which are outside of our control. However, that is why we have dear friends, and we can be one for someone else.

When we feel alone and the world seems full of scary monsters and the roads feel all uphill . . . friends help us see a beautiful valley, an emerald city, and pull back curtains to show us that sometimes those scary things are nothing more than silly perceptions that are actually much smaller than we are.

Great friends have the unique ability to let you know when you are being a "dumb ass," without hurting your feelings or upsetting you in any way! This is totally awesome, by the way, as every now and then, we all get possessed by an idiot and need a friendly reminder to steer us back on the right path!

A true friend would give up the last seat in the lifeboat of the sinking Titanic for you. So better to have one true friend than hundred "sunshine friends" (friends that only come around when times are good). Good friends stand by us as we make both mistakes and achievements, allowing us to learn more about ourselves and our own potential.

When you lose a friend on earth, you add one, to the number of angels that are looking over you.

More often than not, it is sometimes the simplest of things in life that we anxiously wait for, and that becomes our greatest treasure in life . . . like a simple cup of morning coffee shared with a friend.

True, lasting friendships thrive, not because you have found someone who meets your needs, but rather someone who you care enough about having in your life, that you want to do all you can to meet their needs and fill voids in their life! However, as it turns out, when you find that person, you have probably found someone who feels the same way about doing those same acts of kindness for you!

Simple math: one smile + one good laugh + a good friend = a good time and a memory that is sure to last.

A neat thing about good friends is not only can they tell when we are feeling down and blue, excited and glad, or upset and mad . . . not only do they know our emotions they are there to share them with us to help lighten our load!

A true friend will tell you if your morning coffee sucks and then stay and drink two cups of it with you anyway, just for the visit!

When you have someone who stands up for you and defends you and/or your position on something and then never tells you about it, you have found a friend you never want to lose!

When life seems to be "beating you down," call a friend, have a visit, share a drink . . . I guarantee good friends have a "bigger bat" to swing back at "life" than "life" seems to be beating you with!

You know you have a true friend when they will take a call from you while sitting on the toilet. However, always wanting to return the love, and avoid the background noise, I always prefer to tell them the doorbell is ringing and I will have to call them right back!

Good friends are like the little piece of "flint" in a lighter. Without them, we would never get any light; we would just be running around "flicking our bics!"

The awesome thing about great friends is that they always seem to have an extra smile in their pocket for you, just in case, for some reason, you cannot find yours!

Friends are the "security programs" of life that ensure your heart and the "PC" in your brain is protected from the malicious software (words and actions) of others on your hard drive (earth). Be a good friend and make sure in turn that you run "anti-virus" scans regularly on their hearts and "PCs" as well.

Everyone needs to vent frustrations from time to time, that is, if you want to let go of unnecessary stress and prevent a stress-related heart attack! The best of friends just happen to be the best listeners and lets you vent, without judging, without complaining, without trying to fix your every problem, or trying to explain them all away . . . just being there to listen when you need an ear . . . Be that kind of friend, by paying it forward; remember, when someone close to you gets on a soapbox, you can be everything they need you to be by simply giving your time and a *listening* Ear.

The awesome thing about great friends is that they are always what you need them to be. When feeling adventurous, they can be the raft that carries you through the rapids of a strong river. When you need calmness, they are a bridge that you can use to walk across the mighty rapid river!

Learn from the mistakes
of others.
You can't live long
enough to make them
all yourself.

-Eleanor Roosevelt

SECTION TWO

Lighthearted

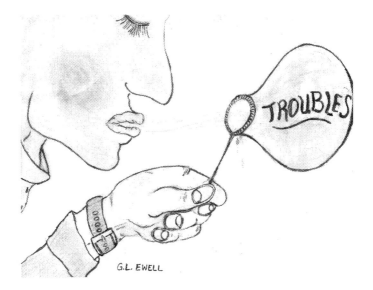

Blowing Troubles Away

Sometimes, you just have to know you can't fix everything at once or some things at all, and put those troubles in a big bubble and blow them away!

I t's not whether you make a big difference or a small one that matters. What matters is that you give of yourself to *make* a difference!

Quite often, dreams are the blueprints of the explorer, inventor, engineer, small business owner, humanitarian, and the handicapped . . . anyone who is seeking for that which does not exist or has yet to be discovered. Things that are currently beyond our reach, which the dreamer believes is within their grasp!

The final result or finished product of something you started cannot always have the happy ending or end up looking exactly as you envisioned in your mind when you started. But as long as you gave 100 percent at the beginning and did your best, right to the end, there is no reason to do anything but hold your head high and be proud of your achievements along the way!

Every day, you will have a positive or negative impact on someone. More often than not, the person whose life you touch will not be the person you are directly interacting with, but someone observing your actions.

A simple act of kindness will make a lasting impression! If nothing else, put on a smile while waiting in a slow checkout line, for your table at a dinner reservation, or to pay for your fuel at a busy convenience store. The domino effect of just one little smile among many impatient frowns is *amazing*!

Because God knew he couldn't be all places at all times, he gave everyone their own special angel to celebrate, live, love, and laugh with, someone to be there in times of sorrow, heartache, and pain . . .

and he simply called them friends. Some so unique, he gave them four legs.

You may be the fastest thoroughbred race horse in the country, but you will never win a race if you waste your time hanging out with a herd of jackasses.

People are often like magnets . . . to surround yourself with people you like, be like "that person" to others!

Whether we want to believe it or not, people are put in our lives for a reason . . . just at the time we need them most. If they stay or go, is not as relevant as that we appreciate them while they are in our lives. It is not important to try to figure out the reason "why" either. To do that is just to waste time that could be better spent enjoying them while we have the chance.

Although these are thought of year round, the holidays that come and go, just seem to reinforce the knowledge that the most precious things in life cannot be built by hand or bought by man: freedom, the ability to see, hear, touch, and feel the beauty of the world around us; to laugh; to enjoy the laughter and smiles of children; the warmth that comes after a small act of kindness for another, a phone call from a best friend; a companion; to love and be loved . . . and God's Love.

If you can't keep your word, perhaps the next most honorable thing you could do, is keep silent rather than committing to a verbal trust you will inevitably alienate.

When your thoughts are of others before yourself, it is nearly impossible for your actions, and the ripple effect from them, to be anything but positive and wonderful.

Often, some of the biggest actions and deeds of the most noble of men have begun with equally big amounts of self-control.

Storms come and go in life . . . with the weather, in your mind, even in your heart. But never do they last forever, and never does one end in your life that there is not a rainbow that follows . . . one is always there, if you look hard enough for it, and a happy, "sunny day" is always sure to follow as well.

Duty, honor, country . . . is not just spoken, but shown in actions, as a true leader does, for others to emulate.

It is a great student that recognizes, learns from, and appreciates a great teacher; and in turn teaches others.

Some of life's greatest teachers afford us the opportunity to learn about one of life's most important subjects: . . . ourselves!

If it is man-made and flies of its own power across the sky, travels across the land on rails, roads, or cables, or crosses vast oceans or up and down mighty rivers to connect people to other people, places, things, and commerce, it began as a dream in the mind of a believer, an adventurer, or an inventor. It failed the first time; they were laughed at, scorned, and ridiculed by others.

Do not be afraid to dream or to chase your dreams, or be too quick to make fun of or belittle someone else. If you can dream it, and want it bad enough, you can make it a reality!

To laugh is to shatter the silence of the mundane in our lives with a joyful "exclamation point," to testify the importance of the "lighter side of life."

One zebra said to the other, "I am white with black stripes," to which another zebra said, "You are not. You are black with white stripes!" A leopard, which overheard them argue about it long enough, said, "You are both wrong. You are so special you are patterns, not colors. You are striped, and both are very special, for no two have stripes just exactly alike. Just as I am neither yellow nor black but spotted, with no one having spots exactly the same as mine! Even those who cannot see colors will know that you are not Donkeys but Zebras. They will know I am not a panther or cougar but a Leopard." It is the pattern of our stripes and spots that make us special, *not* the color of them!

A smile is the conductor of the orchestra of laughter, which plays ballads of joy, composed by the heart.

The truth is, I think, everybody is a little "nuts!" The beauty of it is that not everyone is a peanut, a walnut, pistachio, almond, or a cashew. In a mixed bag of nuts, there is always a particular kind of nut that someone likes and enjoys!

Giving someone a smile is a good way to start the day. The very first person you need to give a great big smile is the person who looks back at you when you first glance into the bathroom mirror, for the entire day will revolve around this person, beginning with this first smile.

Putting on your best smile in the morning certainly won't change the world. However, I guarantee it will make a big impact on your little corner of it and to everyone you cross paths with today!

It is true that there are two sides to every argument. What is not true, however, is that one is right and one is wrong. They could both be right or wrong. What is true is that there are two different perspectives to a situation or perceived thought. Before you dig in your heels and put up barriers to prepare to defend your position, try looking the problem from a different point of view. You just may find out that you are arguing for the same thing just presenting it differently!

I built a climbing wall in my garage. Trust me, it's primitive and not much to look at, but it's safe. I had my princesses and a special friend and her kids over for a visit. Watching the fun they had playing together and climbing all over that wall was like having them climb all over my heart! It made for some awesome memories that couldn't make a Monday start out better! My point is, it doesn't matter how primitive or simple your playtime is with children. All that matters is that you invest the time to play with them.

I love kindness math! For instance, say, one person does one act of kindness, unknowingly witnessed by two people. They are so inspired that they each, in turn, did just one act of kindness within two hours, which was again witnessed by just two people, who in turn each did just one act of kindness within two hours that again (you get it by now) . . . if this little scenario repeated itself just six times . . . just six times . . . in only twelve hours, that first original one simple act of kindness would have turned into 128 acts of kindness in a twelve-hour day! Imagine the impact, if not just one but fifty people did this in your neighborhood, or community every day! So many good deeds, all because one person started the day with something as simple as a kind word, a compliment, or a smile. Imagine!

The best way to prepare to make any day one of the best days of your life is by, right after getting out of bed, putting on your best smile! It goes with everything in your wardrobe, so everything after that is irrelevant.

Sometimes, the very best money you could ever spend is not for a service itself, but rather on the gratuity for the person who provided it.

If someone tries to tell you that things are always right or wrong, or black and white, look to the horizon for the sunrise. There is always color in it and the hope of a fresh new day. Remember, people once told a man the world was flat too!

If you mean it, say it. If you say it, take credit and responsibility for it. Once it leaves your mouth, it is too late to take it back. So if you don't want to take a second and think about it first, be prepared to spend some time after, either explaining it or apologizing for it. Either way, be a big enough person to acknowledge your comments, good, bad, or indifferent.

We know life will throw us a curve ball now and then, yet we stand in the batter's box and wait for the perfect fastball to swing away at . . . yet there are no perfect fastballs in life.

I have heard some say talking to yourself is a sign you might be "losing your mind." I have heard others comment that it is okay; it is when you start answering yourself and talking back to yourself that you need to "look out!" I say as long as you are giving and receiving good advice in your conversations, talk away!

The very brightest of days begins in your heart, not with the weather!

Patriotism is a beautiful thing, born in your heart, nurtured in your mind, and ever ready to be protected with all the strength of one's body. It is also a beautiful thing to assemble, share, talk about, and freely express one's pure "love of county" with other patriots.

Everyone has a story. Everyone has something to give. Everyone has a way to show another that they care. Sometimes, all it takes to lift someone up, or be lifted up, is to take a moment to open your heart and *listen* to the kindness that someone is willing to share.

If good manners were more often practiced and taught, merging onto and off the busy freeway of one's everyday life would feel practically seamless.

Be a bright star, like one in the omnipotent beauty of a majestic night sky away from the lights of the city . . . and be proud of the space you occupy in your own constellation. Although shooting stars can be exhilarating to see; remember, they burn out in the blink of an eye. Choose rather to stay in orbit and let your inner beauty shine so brightly that you may be a beacon of light and a source of inspiration for many, not just for the blink of an eye, but rather a lifetime to love. To wish upon a star is only foolish if you leave your words a wish and do not try to chase them with your actions.

It is good for a man to have a good friend who knows their way around a kitchen rather than the garage. Why? Because when you need it, it hurts a lot less to get smacked with a Teflon cooking spatula than a twelve-inch crescent wrench!

We have invented, created, and mass-produced ways to sail us across vast oceans and to race us from coast to coast over land by road or rail, have conquered the sky and travel among clouds, and even propelled men to the moon. But nothing can take us farther faster than that which was created for us, if used properly . . . a sound mind and a kind heart.

At the end of the day, it does not matter how tired you are when you climb into bed, how little sleep you will get, or how great your successes or failures during the day . . . what matters is that your head can hit the pillow with a smile, knowing throughout the day, you gave your best and perhaps even made someone else laugh or smile along your way.

You can feel a person's true wealth, by the warmth of friendship, the beauty of inner peace and contentment, as well as the self-satisfaction and confidence they radiate when you are near them.

While we cannot change the environment we step into as we walk out our front door for the day, the attitude we walk outside our door with can definitely make a difference and make an impact on those we cross paths with as we go about our day in that environment. Try to add a warm smile to it!

A smile is simply the way your heart "winks" to express joy, and flirt with the beauty it is grateful for at any given moment in time.

A dream is but a wish turned into a sub-conscience blueprint that the conscience mind has access to. A blueprint that because of freedom, if you want it bad enough, "Lady Liberty" will provide you all the resources you need. So what are you waiting for . . . believe in yourself, smile, and make your dream come true!

One only resorts to name calling when there is a lack of intelligence to bring forward anything else of substance, worthy of consideration in a discussion. In those times, it is best to just let go of the conversation, for to follow suit in a reply only proves a lack of intelligence on both sides of the coin.

When all else fails and you feel it's time to break the glass labeled "in case of emergency," as your last resort . . . remember, you still have someone who cares about you . . . weekends . . . and chocolate!

If you want incredible and awesome results, you need to begin with the attitude that you are going to put an incredible and awesome amount of effort into it! Effort does not grow interest. You get back exactly what you are willing to put into something—exercise, play, work, friendships, life, family, or love!

Sometimes, the best rebuttal in argument or difference of opinion, with a person or a group is silence. Not that you could not engage in and tilt the scales in your favor with words of wisdom, first-hand knowledge, or facts, but it is just that sometimes your quiet actions in taking a stand is a more powerful statement than any words wasted on those with whom they would fall on deaf ears anyway.

I get so upset that news agencies cannot seem to get their headlines correct. For the simple truth is gun violence is not on the rise. Idiot violence with a gun however . . . well, just my opinion, but we seem to be producing enough of them, that we should have a surplus to be able to ship overseas to make up for the loss of other commodities, like steel, that we no longer have contributing to our gross national product sales.

Sometimes, when something you really care about is lost, the best way to replace it isn't by rushing out to get a new one. Rather, give something of yourself to others. You might just find what comes back to you will fill the void of your own loss several times over. "Care and Share!"

Every season of the year, and of life for that matter, has a distinct beauty shared by no other. So enjoy every second of it while you can, for before you realize it, it will come to an end, and though it may be replaced, it will never be replicated again once it has passed.

E-books now make up over 25 percent of all the major publishers' profits . . . thick book stock, binding appreciation, and the smell of fresh print, will soon be appreciations lost to the digital age. The roses are still out there in full bloom. The only thing missing is the number of people who will stop long enough to smell and appreciate them.

Ever felt like someone was watching you? Alone in the house this morning, I felt like that. As I got up for a fresh cup of coffee, outside the door going onto my back deck, which my computer desk is right by, I noticed I had friends over for coffee. Two deer were standing on my back deck looking in at me like they were enjoying an exhibit they had just purchased a ticket for. It's always nice to have friends over for coffee.

Often after a storm, you look and look for a rainbow, knowing one is promised, but you do not see one. Yet often, we are pleasantly surprised when without looking for it, a beautifully omnipotent rainbow will appear right before our eyes and take our breath away. They are always there. Sometimes, you just have to look with your heart to see them, rather than your eyes.

It's not just about looking into the mirror as you are preparing to begin or end your day . . . it's about looking into the mirror as you do, and being able to be proud of the person looking back at you!

I believe for the most part people have an inherent goodness about them. If they would let it shine, it would appeal to others, and give them all the self-confidence and friends they desired. This is why I do not understand why so many people feel like the only way to make themselves look good is by putting others down; rather than just showing off their own strengths and willingness to do good works.

To forgive shows compassion of the heart. To forget is a careless way to risk repeating important life lessons, if what is learned is not implemented to keep you from repeatedly making the same mistakes.

When life serves up a great big giant "soup sandwich" to you, don't try to eat it with your hands! Turn things around by dropping it in a bowl, throw in a few crackers, and eat it with a spoon like an awesome "scrumdillyumptious" bowl of stew on a chilly day.

I believe sunrise and sunset are both gifts, one for encouragement to be excited to do good works throughout the day and the other as a thank-you, a reward if you will, for seeking out the opportunities, and doing those good works and kind deeds.

Everyone has within them a positive energy and an inner beauty, complete with wonderful talents and gifts which they can use to pass along and share their inner beauty and that positive energy with others whose lives it could brighten, light up, and even change. There is also a negative energy and all the tools that accompany it. We all can choose which we share with others. To unlock and share the positive is easy, for one to unlock the trunk that contains it, all one has to do is smile. To unlock the other is harder, for the key to it begins with hate, jealously, selfishness, or greed. If you try to start your day with a smile, you will find you will have misplaced the keys to the "other" trunk!

If it makes you smile, it is worth the moment. If it makes you laugh, it is worth your time. If it makes your heart warm, it is worth hanging on to! If it makes you want more, it is joy. If it makes you remember over and over and want more, don't let it go! If it makes you cry, you are either sad you can no longer hold and feel it or upset, that you wasted so much of your time on it. But in all cases, if you spend too much time trying to decide its place and worth, you will have lost it, or didn't need it to begin with.

The last several years, a dear friend has helped me understand that which matters most must pass through your heart before it passes through your pen.

Smiles come straight from the heart. That is why the corners of your mouth are pushed "UP!"

People come and go throughout our lives . . . and while we may not have control over who comes into our lives, we certainly can control who stays in our lives!

Never pass up an opportunity to open a window or blind and let a ray of sunshine brighten your room . . . you'll find it not only brightens the room, but it will brighten and warm your heart as well, if you'll let it.

Life is too short to try to mold someone to complement your heart. If they aren't perfect from the start, they will not be a perfect fit a month, a year, or even ten from now.

Dance through life if you can. Waltz in the past to soak in its memories. Tango in the future with zest and a spice for adventures in life ahead. But slow dance today and savor every minute, for today's dance is the only one you know for certain, that you will have to hear the music of.

We will never get all that we want from life. However, we all have the ability to make all we want out of whatever life gives us.

Kindness is so easy. It rarely requires more than a smile, engaging your mind before running your mouth and simply listening to what others have to say with an open heart.

Awesome mothers are the chorus line to "Songs of Success, Achievement and Love," that children sing in their hearts every day, regardless their age!

A walk under the vast omnipotent beauty of a perfectly clear night sky, away from the lights of the city, not only takes your breath away but also replaces it with sweet breath of mother nature, to fill your lungs and free the clutter of the day from your mind . . . so you can focus on a magical walk.

You are as young as you desire to be; the physical condition in which you maintain your body and allow your heart to feel are important factors. Age does not matter and, in fact, is not a factor at all! For remember, age is nothing more than a measurement of time. It is not a physical attribute! So do something fun, spontaneous, and laugh out loud funny with a friend . . . and see if you don't feel ten years younger!

You can never judge a person's true wealth by looking at their material gains. You cannot drive "happiness." One cannot water-ski behind "true love." You cannot gain interest in any bank account, mutual fund, or IRA from the "smiles of children." It is impossible to improve or get a better credit rating by "volunteering" your time to help improve the quality of life of others, and "trust" is something that can never be demanded or simply bought and hung on a wall to display for guests. You can tell if your day has started out on the right foot by the smiles on the faces of those around you . . .

Aspire to reach the top of your own personal summit and to stay there not letting anyone knock you down. Remember, it is from the top of the summit, not the bottom, that you have the farthest sight and ability to see things as they are to help yourself and others and find your own personal happiness.

There is good reason why you don't stand on the very top of the ladder! It is also probably strongly encouraged for blind guys not to use ladders! Just saying . . . however, when my head quits hurting, I will use the pull-up bar I installed over my back door and do pull-ups every time I enter or exit the house! I will get stronger!

This kid is taking over his corner of the world. So look out. One person's freedoms or security being violated is one too many! It starts now! "random acts of violence" are going to be replaced with "random acts of kindness!" Just try to stop me!

When it feels like you have hit bottom and the world is still throwing shovels at you, you don't need to wait for a "sign" that things will get better. All it takes is a little bit of faith in yourself! By the way, you can also use all the shovels as props to help you climb *up and out* of the hole; not just for digging!

Today, I am not going to worry about the spineless, gutless, no conscience, two-faced, anti-constitutional, lying, money-grabbing, lobbyist-owned, career politician bastards that make up the majority of our congress. Instead, I think I will pray to a God I know exists to bless those in office who do represent the people and care about our constitution and who themselves pray to their God to help them make wise decisions for America. I will also pray for our brave servicemen and women still in harm's way. Then I believe I will clean my guns, with a smile on my face, knowing that they are one of the greatest inventions in history and that they are a good thing that unfortunately sometimes stupid people get their hands on . . . much like automobiles and drunk drivers. Then I think I will go to "Mickey D's" and get a Big Mac, a large order of fries, and cover them with loads of salt and extra fry sauce, simply because I can and I am not afraid too; and two large cokes, since they quit selling a super-sized one, caving in to government pressure. Not that I do not believe in eating healthy food, I just disagree with the government trying to "regulate" what I eat. Then I think I will walk around and smile at people and give them a nice greeting for no other reason than being polite and friendly. I will open a door for a woman not because I think women are weak but because I believe in showing women respect; and don't believe being a gentleman should ever go "out of style." I will pause to appreciate the beauty around me. I will make time to listen to my children; walk the dog, and do some house work or yard maintenance; send an e-mail to my congressman; because I believe that my opinion matters and does make a difference; and pick a friend to call just to say hello.

"Old Glory" has not burned out. Everything our flag represents remains intact to the American Patriot. I pray I use each day to do good works and be a better citizen so that my stitch in the flag remains tight and strong.

Whether your attire is your very best formal suit or dress, casual wear, or work clothes, there is nothing you can choose to accessorize or complement any outfit for wear better than a smile.

Open the window to your heart often to let beauty and kindness in. However, make sure you keep the screen in the window, as there are those who would try to push through ugly bitterness and hatred as well.

If you can start your Friday with a big smile, chances are it will end with one . . . which is the perfect way to slide into the weekend!

When you stand up for what is right, you can never be wrong, no matter how you are standing. With the will and courage to stand, your posture can never be criticized.

Sometimes, I think we all see and hear things for reasons we know and understand yet choose to ignore if it is not exactly what we thought we would see or hear.

No matter how you are dressed or what your outfit looks like, if you accessorize it with a smile, you will always be dressed for any occasion!

Perception really is everything. So don't hesitate to pause and take a second look at any given situation anytime at all.

Sometimes, you just need to sit down and laugh or cry . . .

The Trouble is,
You THINK you have
Time.
        -Buddha

In this life we cannot always
    do great things,
but we can do small things
    with great love.
        - mother Theresa

SECTION THREE

Volunteering and Time

Grandfather of Time

The only time you will never question if you have wasted is
time you spend doing random acts of kindness for others.

M ore often than not, if you wait for those who truly need your help to ask you specifically for it, you just as well put your gloves away, as you will never use them.

Only you know to what extent you may be able to do for someone. If you see someone in need of something you can provide, don't be afraid to offer it. If you don't, helping someone might end up nothing more than a nice passing thought that you had.

Angels are among us everywhere. You won't find them looking for wings and halos, but rather by noticing the kind deeds they selflessly perform for others every day. You might also recognize them by the name they go by here on earth: *volunteers*.

The blind have learned to see without eyes. The deaf have learned to hear without ears. A double amputee can embrace someone without arms. The mute can communicate without a voice. It is all about heart! Hearts can connect, embrace, see, and communicate in a second language that everyone knows and has the potential to be fluent in.

Be your own ambassador for love and kindness. Open your heart and help others. Be a volunteer. Donate a little money to a charity you like. Open you heart and see, hear, embrace, communicate, and enjoy this beautiful world like never before!

In today's world, it is not merely enough to agree or disagree with something. If you want to make a difference, get involved! Pick "anything" you believe in, and then put down the smart phone for a measly hour . . . I promise the world will not end without you getting a text about it, in one hour. For one hour, volunteer your time, energy, and resources (without your smart phone) to do something good for another person, animal, place, or thing and see if you don't feel "better off" for have taken the time to make the investment.

If your heart is in the right place, more often than not, your mind and helping hands will be also.

No one can get through every battle in their life with just one hand. However, it only takes one hand to reach out to someone in need or to grab the hand of someone reaching out to you to instantly double the odds of winning every battle.

Acts of kindness are not measured by what you do, but rather *that* you do.

There comes a time in every one's life when they realize, though their intentions were good, they were hatched from an overzealous desire to want to jump in and help someone who we hear is struggling on the path they are traveling in life only to realize they were coming out of a "stormy sea" when we jumped in and knocked them back into it.

It is a noble thing to want to help others. It is the right thing only when you know that your jumping to someone's aid will actually put you a position to pull them to shore, not land on and push them underwater.

I love every opportunity I get to talk to people and let them know how much I appreciate their own individual patriotism and how truly grateful I am for their support of our servicemen and women and our veterans!

Our nation's flag is dear to my heart. So too is everything it represents and symbolizes! I am so grateful for our freedoms, and the giving, inspiring spirit of passionate volunteers! If you are one of our rare and tireless volunteers . . . I salute you! I am grateful for you, and most of all, I want to say thank you!

In times of trouble, everyone is afraid of something or for someone! Some are afraid for themselves and run; some are afraid and confused and end up freezing in a state of shock; and then there are the precious few who are afraid for others and failure and neither run away nor freeze, but square their shoulders and move steadfast and with purpose toward the danger! They are determined to give their all to protect and to serve, with precious resolve to make a difference, regardless of any personal sacrifice or price that is paid as they use their fear as an endorsement to step up and do the right thing!

When you strive to help others and smile from your heart, others smile with you; noticing your good works, not whether or not your teeth are straight!

If collectively we all try to do just one little thing every day to give just one person a reason to smile or laugh, imagine the impact it could have on everyone and everything around us.

The country/world needs more knights. Rather, men to act with the moral courage, conviction, and desire to do noble works and deeds as the fabled knights of King Arthur's Round Table. Knights who would follow his fabled code of chivalry "we are nobles as long as we are sought out; the greater the bounty we may give, the greater our nobility, fame, and honor." No doubt the more we can afford to give of ourselves, the greater the feeling of joy in our hearts

It doesn't matter whether you are a knight in shining armor or if your armor is tarnished, dented, and marred with scars of battle. In fact, whether you have armor at all is irrelevant. All that matters is your willingness to help others whenever and wherever you can. Seeing the smiles on the faces of those you help will leave you feeling like a noble knight.

More often than not, all that is required of us to help solve someone else's problems is simply to be a good listener.

Often, one of the best things we can do to help others is some "self-improvement." Whether we work to become physically stronger, mentally stronger, or spiritually stronger, the stronger we become, the more stamina and endurance we will have to help others.

If we let it, our heart will emit a bright light of love that will enable us to see more of those we may be in a position to help, as we travel along the path of our own individual journeys through life. I truly believe the more of our brothers and sisters that we can help along our way, the smoother our own path will be further on down the road.

To give of ourselves, our time, money, or other resources to another is more than just an offering of hope or gesture of gratitude and of caring for the receiver. It is also a validation to ourselves that we are healthy, wealthy, and wise enough to share some our good fortune with another who does not have our same abilities at the time. When the day comes we no longer have a desire to help, give, or volunteer, it is not those in need we have given up on, it is us.

Who cares if you put your "best foot forward," and someone criticizes your non-matching socks! The good that can come from it and the feeling you get in your heart will enable you to laugh it off and even feel bad for the critic that would rather judge your clothing than roll up their sleeves and lend someone a helping hand!

If the government knew just how powerful and contagious and awesome the feeling is when we do good works and help others truly, they would either try to harness that good, powerful energy for a bomb or try to tax it.

Time will never slow down long enough to ask you if you would like it, or it will not allow some "extra time" for you to give of yourself to others. However, if on your own, you make the time to give of yourself, your talents, your knowledge, or your help and aid to others, I guarantee that you will find you have all the time in the world to perform any, and as many, act of kindness as you would like to start!

It is important to invest time with a dear friend or loved one, as these precious memories are treasures that even "time" cannot take away from you. Some of the best memories you can make together is by volunteering together to perform a service project to help another in need.

Time has a way of erasing away the trivialities and mundane of our everyday lives, as we have no reason to hang onto that which is irrelevant. Another way to eliminate the mundane in our lives is to fill the void by volunteering.

So many charities are looking for donations this time of year (the holiday season). Most of them are legitimate; some are not. So many people are out with their "Need Money" or "Need Food" signs (I haven't seen any that say "Want Work!"). Some of them are legitimate; most are not. One thing to remember, if you feel inclined to donate, is that if all you have is pocket change, or even a dollar, never feel embarrassed or ashamed to donate anything! Every little bit helps, and it all adds up! The "legitimate charities" are just as happy for a $1.00 donation as they are for a $20.00 donation, and just as grateful! If you can, give.

You don't have to climb Mt Everest to feel on top of the world. In fact, you don't have to climb at all. Simply do something kind for someone in need who could really use your help!

It is better to have a heart
without words
Than words without heart.
— Mahatma Gandhi

Anyone can be passionate,
but it takes real lovers
to be silly.
— Rose Franken

SECTION FOUR

Love

Trampled Hearts Still Love

Even the most trampled on heart will once again radiate
light if it is tenderly loved.

L ove runs on its own time. It can be sought after, chased, coaxed, longed for, and desired. However, only when it is ready will it happen; and then, whether you are ready for it or not, it will bloom. It is then up to you to maintain it. If nurtured and nourished, it will blossom and bloom forever. If ignored, it will quickly fade away, wither up, wilt, and die.

The price of mailing parcels from the U.S. Postal Service (USPS) went up. However, there are still two items that can be shipped via same day air-mail free of charge to any destination in the world: kisses and hugs. Both can still be tossed on the wind to a loved one for free, and they always get to their destination on time.

What makes something special is not its cost. It doesn't matter if it's a one of a kind. It's not if it's the best on the market, the very latest technology, the biggest, fastest, brightest, or the most exotic. What makes anything special is simply the value or meaning it has in your heart and the memories attached to it; it is love. If it is something that you love, it is something that is priceless!

You can wish upon a star, throw a penny in a fountain or a horseshoe over your shoulder, even put a rabbit's foot in your pocket, or find a four-leafed clover. But if it's love you're wishing for, it never will come true without applying a little faith and daring to share a little of your heart with that someone who is very special to you!

There is no harbor in the world that the illuminating, bright light of love cannot cut through the darkness to ensure every vessel that someone cares about can find safe passage through rocks, reefs, and sandbars to safely dock at the port of the one whose love showed them the way!

To truly love someone or something requires one thing in its simplest form. That one thing is simply on a regular basis, prioritizing someone else's wants, needs, and desires above your own! If you focus on someone else's happiness before your own, the surprise is that you will find you end up feeling like you are the one whose happy meter is "pegged!"

If the sun shines brightly in your own heart, its rays of happiness will radiate and brighten someone else's heart along your travels.

Everyone has an opinion. Everyone has something to contribute and share. Everyone has feelings, and everyone the ability to care. The key is to actively listen and process all the information with not just your head but your heart. If we would all try to understand the viewpoints of others and throw out bias, the past, and "hate-rooted" remarks, there would be much less apathy and animosity toward each other, and many more good decisions we each make from the start.

The sunroof to your heart is opened with a smile.

True love is found not where bodies physically collide, but rather where hearts and souls entwine.

"What goes around comes around . . ." usually a saying associated in a negative light or as a saying of revenge. However, just think what a wonderful saying and thing it would be if "What goes around . . ." *started* with *love!*

Sometimes on the darkest of nights, the light of love can be found shining brightest from the eyes of a dear friend sent to light your path.

The heart of a loved one may be a great distance away with your eyes open, but with your eyes closed, you can almost feel their heart beat next to you.

If you are determined to see things begin and end with love, the filling in between can be nothing but wonderful.

Love knocks or calls often when you least expect it and quietly and gently comforts you like a warm blanket on a chilly morning. It gives and takes, but it is not selfish, in that it never takes more than it gives, when it is both given and received first from your heart.

Love = Listening Openheartedly Very Essential.

What makes people gravitate toward others that they would like to be around? If you take a closer look, I believe you will find it is *not* money, stocks, or large estates. I believe you will find it is laughter, kindness, and love.

Most everything a person owns can be taken from them. However, memories and love locked in your heart, not a single soul can steal.

I believe the reason a rainbow has so many different colors is it reflects the diversity and love that not only should we embrace within each other, but the love that the creator of that rainbow has for every one on the earth. There is a color for everyone, and love is what makes them all so omnipotent!

A lover or loved one is often a sound board to emphasize or reinforce things we can do to touch the hearts of others in ways that do not hurt feelings . . . and living life is the only "lab" that affords us to test our actions and get the feedback we need to learn and grow.

The embers of a fire are not a sign that the fire is about to die, but rather an indicator that the fire is very much alive and available if we still desire its open flame. So too are embers within us, in hearts or minds, available and capable of burning brightly again. But it is up to us to feed them.

Love . . . if it is not unconditional, you have mistaken it for something else.

When you find it hard to leave someplace or someone you have been visiting, you know it is someplace special, people dear to your heart, and a place to return to as soon as you can.

What you pass along will return to you. Perhaps that is why it eludes so many. It is such an easy formula; our human tendencies muck it up by trying to make it more complicated than simply loving yourself and passing that love along to others. Test it out. Smile at yourself in the mirror, and then smile at a stranger along your way . . . see if you don't get a smile back. The secret is, there isn't a secret. Just share a little bit of the love that starts with you.

When we open our hearts and give a little of ourselves to others, we make room for the abundance of love that will come back to us . . . enough to fill the void we created and then some, with plenty leftover to give again.

Some hurts you just can't fix for others. You can't wrap them, splint them, or find a Band-Aid or roll of gauze big enough to cover them. For those hurts, the best you can do is to put your arms around the person hurting and let a soft spoken word and your heartfelt love do what it can.

A heart filled with love gives off warmth that everyone can feel!

With love, you can find even more love if you simply take the time to nurture and appreciate that which your heart is telling you pay attention to!

The loving and unprejudiced heart can make the right decision long before the uneducated mind that waits without faith for facts.

When you miss someone bad enough to hurt and so much that you feel whole only when you are together . . . you know you have stumbled upon one of life's secrets.

You may not find the strength to say it, but there is no reason why you can't write it down for someone you care about to read, "I Love You!" You never know, you would hate to find yourself saying . . . "If only I . . ."

Just as no skilled tradesman only has one tool in their toolbox, no one person has every skill, talent, or experience needed to help you through all the trials of your life. Therefore, embrace everyone who comes into your life with love and friendship. You just never know who will possess the "tool" you need to get you through a rough spot on the path you are traveling through life.

When you lose someone very dear to you, remember when treated with nothing but love, kindness, and honesty, the amount of time you know someone has nothing to do with the void they leave in your heart!

Act to provide comfort and help or to protect others is not a sign of our generosity or ability to help. Neither should it ever be a chance to "grab a headline". Rather, it is testament to one's character, but not for others to judge. Rather, for ourselves to be able to ask and answer in our own hearts, "Did I do *all* that I could do, given the situation or circumstance, to make a substantial difference with this opportunity I was gifted with?" It is with a solemn humbleness and a pure inner peace when we can answer . . . *yes!* There is an inner chamber of sadness when we know we could have done more and held back. A learning curve not lost, if we seek to provide when able, before we find ourselves in a situation wishing others would have done more, if you are ever on the receiving end of an act of charity . . . which is pure love from the heart.

You can say it over and over and over again . . . but until you show it, and feel it one time, it really has no meaning or value to it all . . . Love.

It is much easier to open your heart to love and charity once you have opened your mind to being a broker of kindness and feeling the desire in in your heart to want to help others. You just never know, out of a love for spreading kindness, romantic love has also been found!

Love . . . It can't fix everything, but it sure can put a big Band-Aid on anything!

I always thought that love was supposed to be one of the strongest forces in the universe! So why do people seem to not want any part of it? I guess maybe it still is. It sure seems to be able to pick me up and throw me under a bus and left for road kill whenever I think I have stumbled onto it. Who knows, I still believe in "One Day!" If you're still following my posts fifty years from now, I'll let you know whether to believe is "stupidity" or "blind faith!"

Life is like a giant business, our every action, a customer service, or business transaction. Everything we give or receive requires a payment, mostly, in the form of love and kindness. If we pay for services we receive, like love and friendship, with love and kindness, we will get great customer service. If we provide a service, like love and friendship, with sincerity of heart and a true desire to make someone else's day a special one, we will have loyal customers who will ensure our business thrives. Love and kindness, the most effective way to ensure our every transaction is processed, our credit is endless, and our business is always packed with loving and loyal consumers for life!

Love can be desired, sought after, chased, coaxed, persuaded, given, offered, and entrusted, but it cannot be bought!

True love, like a very fine wine, becomes more exquisite and exotic as it ages, if it is handled properly and with care.

The hearts of lovers are very fragile. They can withstand a lot of pain, but not without leaving scars that never truly heal. Once hurt, the hurt never truly ever goes away. Handle them with care!

Sometimes, the most powerful and remembered conversations between lovers are had when the heart speaks and the mouth is silent.

True love can be communicated through a hug, a kiss, the holding of a hand, or even by just looking into the eyes of the one you love.

How would you explain the beautiful smell of a rose to someone who could not smell or describe the magnificent array of colors in a brilliant sunset to one who has never had sight? How would you relate the sweet taste of sugar to one that has never tasted it? I believe not all things that touch our hearts need words to pass them long. Some things are best conveyed with a simple hug, a tender touch, or an "I Love You!"

Patriotism means
to stand by
the country.
I does not mean
to stand by the
president or
any other
public official.

-Theodore Roosevelt

SECTION FIVE

Military, Government, and Government-Recognized Holidays

My Symbol of Freedom

Our flag, if you want peace in your life, let it blow with everything it represents in your heart!

Halloween, the one day of the year I am not self-conscience about answering the door with my fake eye out of my eye socket.

With Veterans Day over, it is now that time of year, when between now and Thanksgiving, that thirty million turkeys are desperately trying to either walk like a duck or "honk" like a goose.

Perhaps there would be a lot more common sense exercised by congress, if they too had to live by and adhere to all the laws, rules, and legislation they themselves propose, vote on, and pass into law!

Wars and warriors are all too soon forgotten by those not affected by the reality of the price paid by those who courageously and with valor did their duty fighting in them. But to those few who endured, sweat, and bled together, the memories and bonds of "brotherhood" will endure beyond the grave. I hope their hearts find peace long before then.

Much love to those still in harm's way in Afghanistan, still giving their all, for all of us.

American troops are tough, tenacious, and compassionate. No doubt about it, they are strong of heart to endure, persevere, and care.

This time of year, it is always wonderful to see the endless small acts of kindness that people do for each other! It exemplifies what we are all capable of collectively, as we genuinely give a little more, seem to care a little more, and show a little more tolerance and patience with others. One can't help but enjoy the "feel good" that comes from even the smallest of kind acts, something as simple as sharing a smile or letting someone go ahead of you on the freeway or in a checkout line while shopping. The real beauty is, it doesn't have to end with the holiday! Wouldn't it be nice if everyone's "holiday best" toward one another were a standard we all tried to emulate every day of the year, rather than just a few weeks before Christmas?

Wise men looked to the heavens and followed a star. Wise men sought to honor and follow him then, just as wise men seek to follow him now. Another group of wise men and women are deployed to distant lands and stand armed at the gate. They are away from their loved ones, in harsh conditions and doing their best, to ensure that, wise or not, all can enjoy this special holiday within our American borders with those we care about, free of the rampant lawlessness, genocide, and terrors of war that plague other places of the world. God bless them all.

Of all the things I do, talking to elementary school students is definitely one of the most fun and most rewarding. Their innocence, honesty, and imaginations can lead to some challenging, tough, and totally "laugh out loud" questions, all of which warm my heart.

Happy New Year to everyone! It is my wish that the very best of the last year will be the very worst of your New Year!

One thing I would like to recommend to everyone, as you are going about organizing personal files, preparing for tax season, and other miscellaneous "this and that" for the New Year, is to take a couple of minutes to find out who your government leaders are and how to contact them, from your local city government officials, to your state or commonwealth representatives for your district or precinct, and to your national congressional representative and senators. Have a place you can readily find their contact phone numbers and e-mails . . . and then make it a point to use them on occasion, to let them know how you feel on issues important to you. Believe it or not, your e-mails get read, and your voice and opinion does make a difference.

For the "peace" in America we may enjoy, and take for granted, yet another day, thank you my "brothers and sisters" who are still in harm's way, being the barrier which confines evil outside of our borders!

I am very grateful for awesome, hardworking teachers! If we invested in more in our teachers and schools and prioritized education; in the long run, I doubt that there would be the need for as much government spending in defense, criminal justice, and detention programs. Just my opinion . . .

Our nation's most valuable resources require clean air and water daily. They also need to feel loved, hugged, and to sit down with you for a meal and have you listen to them tell you about their day. They need be read to, and have you listen to them read, and have the opportunity to receive a good education. They need to be able to play . . . to be kids and encouraged to explore the world of their imaginations. They need to live each day without fear, at home, at school, and while walking or riding the bus in between. They will be our leaders tomorrow, and if we want good ones, we need to play an active role in providing them with the tools they will need to be good ones. They also need to be protected by those that love and care for them . . . with every asset available to you, and if necessary with the use of force, to whatever degree is required, to ensure that their youth is preserved, they do not become the victims of violence, and evil is eliminated from their little corner of the world, for no child can remain a child, live happy, and learn in an environment where fear is allowed to dominate them.

I didn't sleep well last night, but at least I didn't sleep well in a nice home, in a clean bedroom, in comfortable clothing, in a very large comfortable bed! Thank you my "brothers" for enduring what most can't imagine, in between your missions through hell.

Sometimes, you have to travel 8,000 miles to protect the ones you love, and no matter the hell you found or the hell that found you, you would travel the 8,000 miles over and over and over again to keep them safe.

Homicide rates are lower in history than hundred years ago. What is amazing is that today the population is three times what it was then: according the Census Bureau 1918 pop: 104,550,000; 2010 pop: 308,745,538. You cannot dispute the sheer increase in the number of criminals that three times the population has produced. So why haven't crime rates consistently increased? You can't dispute better law enforcement. However, you cannot discredit either, the fact that responsible gun owners have had a huge impact on lower homicide rates, and crime rates in general, as fewer restrictions have been placed on second amendment rights, especially in the last twenty years.

It's not Veteran's Day or Memorial Day . . . it's a regular everyday type of day, and I just wanted to say thanks. Thank you to all our military service men and women, to all those doing their duty today, to the best of their ability, with courage, honor, and pride so that I could enjoy this day, doing anything I choose to do in a peaceful environment!

Today is National Vietnam Veterans Day (March 29). My dad spent forty-three months in Vietnam. *Welcome home, Dad!* Forty years ago, over 58,000 of America's sons and daughters paid the ultimate price for freedom, and over 300,000 were wounded. They did not come home to parades and banners, flags waving, and a nation proud of them . . . but they damn sure deserved it! Thank you, Dad, and all my "brothers" and "sisters" who endured hell to stop the spread of communism in a foreign land called Vietnam!

Have a ton of fun today! But remember, amid the eggs, chocolate bunnies, and yellow marshmallow "peeps . . ." while enjoying laughter and gatherings with friends and family . . . to take a just a moment and silently remember . . . that the day is also about a man—a carpenter, teacher, fisherman, and soldier, who broke through the barrier of the grave and made it possible for all of us to have a road to travel back "Home," if we wanted to travel that way. Also, just a moment of personal silence, for many of my "brothers and sisters," who are still fighting the "war on terrorism" so that today, in peace, we can enjoy the laughter of those we are sharing the day with. Happy Easter!

The National Medal of Honor day is officially observed on March 25 each year. The Medal of Honor is the highest distinction that can be awarded by the president, in the name of the Congress, to members of the Armed Forces who have distinguished themselves conspicuously by gallantry and intrepidity at the risk of lives above and beyond the call of duty. This day should be one of our most revered. Unfortunately, all too many Americans are not even aware of its existence. For the most part, the occasion comes and goes with little notice. The date of March 25 was chosen because the first Medal of Honors was awarded to members of Andrew's Raiders on March 25, 1863, for their action during the "Great Locomotive Chase."

I truly love, Lady Liberty, and all she stands for and was honored to have been a "Defender of Freedom."

There were many a good argument presented in both houses of congress, for passing legislation to recognize special days, such as President Day, for the country to stop, remember, and be grateful for the unwavering, selfless service and sacrifices these men have made to the preservation of our country and the freedoms they passed on for us, to not only enjoy, but to preserve and protect. Perhaps if everyone actually paused for just a moment to reflect upon and appreciate such selfless service and sacrifice, our hearts, minds, and those of our leaders would be directed to do those things that would continue to protect and preserve them.

President Washington, it's your birthday! Because of your courage, beliefs, and willingness to put your life on the line for us, it is "We the People," who are receiving the gifts! I am sure many of them you spent tired, angry and much alone; as you fought for "our" independence, religious freedoms, individual rights, and a nation to call "Home."

Thank you to my "Sisters in Uniform," mothers, who this day (Mother's Day) are deployed and at war, helping to protect our freedoms, performing their duties with a heart which has a tear upon it, as they cannot be with their children on their "special day!"

Today is Armed forces Day! If given the opportunity, don't pass it by, to thank someone who is currently serving, or has served, in our nations Armed Forces.

Armed Forces Day was first observed on May 20, 1950.

In 1962, President John F. Kennedy established Armed Forces Day as an official holiday (It is observed the third Saturday of May each year). As intended By President Harry S. Truman, today let us all come together to thank our military service members for their faithful service defending and protecting the freedoms we enjoy and, far too often, take for granted.

To my "brothers and sisters" still fighting the war on terrorism, thank you for remembering us at home, even those who have forgotten about you. I won't forget!

It is about time that fifty people step up and put some brakes on an out-of-control train in Washington, D.C. If collectively the governors of each state united with a bold statement that reminded the federal government, they need to start showing more respect to the states, *not* the states showing more fear of the federal government. Just my opinion . . .

We have freedom, thanks to the bravery of our forefathers who believed, fought, and secured it for us. We enjoy it today, because of the bravery and courage of those who have since preserved it. We will enjoy it tomorrow and pass the precious gift of it on to our children, based on our actions and courage now. It is not only preserved with a gun, but at the election booth and with what we teach our children as well, which only we deicide, not the government. Do not forget, there is a good reason that our government is "of the people, for the people."

Some say there are two sides to every story, and the truth is found in the middle. Some will say three, party one, party two, and accounts and facts gathered from evidence and eye witness "perceptions." I think often there is four: party one, party two, the "I watched it all and can tell it all to a TV camera," and the "Oh, I've seen it all but it was none of my business" person. I wouldn't make a good peace officer, because I would arrest everyone who watched and did nothing, before I would arrest anyone else! The safest neighborhoods are the ones where those who live in them are looking out for each other, not the ones where people look the other way thinking it's law enforcement's responsibility to magically appear every time there are problems that wouldn't exist if the people who lived in the area took a stand for right and justice, united to "keep the trash" from collecting, gathering, and piling up in their own corner of the world.

Shit-Bird: Military term of endearment used to express feelings of strong heart-felt emotion toward another service member without risking sounding like a "wussie" in front of others by saying "I love you, man!"

Also: A term used by military members to describe someone who has just "F'd" up beyond all recognition the assignment they were given or expected to carry out for the good of the whole.

It can be used to describe someone who falls under both definitions described above at the same time!

Sir Adrian Paul Ghislain Carton de Wiart is perhaps the toughest "S.O.B." I have ever had the privilege of reading about; in his memoirs, he wrote, "Governments may think and say as they like, but force cannot be eliminated, and it is the only real and unanswerable power. We are told that the pen is mightier than the sword, but I know which of these weapons I would choose."

There is no place in the world or out of it (i.e., Moon) that this flag, our flag, my flag does not wave with the glory of everyone who has fought for it, the humbleness of all who love it, and the reverent spirit of everything that is freedom and peace that it represents! Anyone who thinks otherwise is a hateful, jealous, spiteful soul that tries to attach false labels to it, which simply put are things outside of the umbrella, of the goodness and peace, of all those who believe in her!

Let us not forget the heavy price that has been paid for the upcoming Memorial Holiday.

May I not take today for granted, knowing the seriousness with which others are taking it for me! Thank you all (our military servicemen and women).

This memorial weekend, please take a moment to silently remember and give thanks to those who have unselfishly given and paid the ultimate price for the freedoms we enjoy.

Remember, as well, that with each of them, a family mourns forever, for the void left in their hearts that will always be present, for the loss of their beloved soldier, sailor, and airman or marine.

One just can't argue the simple fact for Switzerland's low gun violence rate . . . nor the fact that individual rights to own guns was so important, it was the second amendment to our constitution!

When you hear about a broadside bomb (an IED—improvised explosive device; or an EFP—explosive formed projectile . . . the real bad boys) being detonated on our troops in Afghanistan, do not for a second believe, that was the only bomb set out for the day. In Iraq in late 2006, we were averaging over 3,100 bomb incidents a month, an incident being one we found or one that found us. Over one hundred bombs a day . . . *every day!* Imagine just for a moment, taking your chances on your morning commute, hoping like hell to dodge one hundred bombs! Our "Route Clearance" teams do an excellent job and find over 90 percent of them before they unleash their death upon and fury on anything in their way. Just one kills or cripples a soldier forever. Imagine the death toll if we were only finding 10 or 20 percent of these deadly instruments of war!

God bless our servicemen and women! Every last one of them! From yesterday, today, or tomorrow; they all deserve a "thank-you" for giving all of us their best . . . "Thank you!"

Let us humbly take just a second every day to remember that while we are here at home enjoying our freedoms, 8,000 miles away young American servicemen and women are paying the ultimate price for them! May who loved them and are without them now know our humble gratitude and sorrow for their loss.

What makes a soldier push forward with courage and stand tall with valor; and endure; maintain; sustain; never give up, and never say die? The humble strength that comes from within a soldier's heart!

Today in 1990, The Supreme Court struck down a federal law prohibiting desecration of the American flag. A sad day and pathetic ruling from the court, not to protect the flag I love and fought so dearly to protect. Once the symbol of our country fell, God has become the next target. Taken out of federal buildings, out of our schools, out of Christmas scenes, and now even off our money! And now second amendment rights to strip away . . . what sadly will be tomorrows, today?

We still have over 56,000 (source wiki.answers.com) in harm's way, fighting terrorism in Afghanistan. Please do not forget my "brothers and sisters" there who are fighting for you.

The soldier presses forward ignoring hunger and pain. What they are protecting is not personal glory or fame!

The war on terrorism is not over! Remember, there are still over 56,000 (source wiki.answers.com) military service members in Afghanistan still fighting in America's longest war, in the terrorist's homeland, to ensure they are kept at bay, and not doing their dirty deeds in our homeland!

I am an American, and I am free today because someone fought, bled, or died in my place. I vow that as long as there is breath in my body that their sacrifice will not be in vain.

Though America's birthday is now over, every day, I will be grateful for the umbrella of freedom she provides me! So remember well "Don't Tread on Me" and "This We Will Defend," because another statement many of us believe in is, "Give Me Liberty or Give Me Death."

In a perfect world keeping the peace would be as easy as smiling at the person you are interacting with. In the often violent society in which we live, unfortunately, sometimes I can smile because I am grateful for those who are not afraid to interact and intervene with those who would seek to harm others and take away their smile, often by communicating with violent offenders in the only language they understand . . . a loaded weapon. Thank you to soldiers and law enforcement officials and educated armed civilians, who are not afraid to do a job others are not willing to do, to ensure the rest of us can live in an environment where we can share our smiles with others.

Sixty-eight years ago, WWII ended . . . the median age of the WWII soldier was twenty-four. Let's say twenty-two to make the math easy . . . 68 + 22 = 90, which if living would be the average age of the WWII veteran. Sad to think how very few of the greatest generation of WWII veterans are still with us. Each of them is a living library of history to be visited and listened to, while we still have a few to give us a first-hand account of history!

Labor Day is a national holiday, and creation of the labor movement, that pays tribute to the contributions workers have made to the country. Oregon was the first state to make it a holiday on February 21, 1887. It became a federal holiday in 1894 to all those who "build America" and keep her running—American craftsmen, road and bridge builders, utility workers, agricultural workers, miners, union workers—to all who labor and keep America strong by "the sweat of their brow." As a soldier, a veteran, and wounded warrior, I salute you, and thank you!

A true warrior longs for the day they can lay down their weapon and live in peace. However, they know it cannot happen, for when not used in war to protect, it must be used in peace, to remain proficient and retain skills needed to be victorious at war!

In the United States, Armed Forces Day is celebrated on the third Saturday in May. Thank You, from my heart, to all of our military "Defenders of Freedom!"

Memorial Day is observed every year in the United States on the final Monday of May.

Veterans Day is observed on November 11 of each year. Veterans Day is also the anniversary of the end of World War I. World War I was formally ended at the eleventh hour of the eleventh day of the eleventh month of 1918, when the armistice with Germany went into effect.

Veterans Day is not to be confused with Memorial Day; Veterans Day celebrates the service of all U.S. military veterans, while Memorial Day is a day of remembering the men and women who died while serving.

You cannot hang out with negative people and expect to live a positive life.

—Joel Osteen

SECTION SIX

Spiritual and Self-help

G.L. EWELL

Iron Cross

When you work hard for something in life and obtain it, an education, career progression, love . . . when you obtain it, you appreciate it and are not careless to let it slip away. When one expects life to deliver happiness to their doorstep without working and giving for it . . . life is a disappointment, and happiness long sought after won't ever be won permanently.

Sometimes, it is not possible or conceivable to let go of fear that a person may have about any given event, activity, or circumstance they might find themselves in. It is, however, possible to turn that fear into a positive energy that can help you stay focused, alert, and achieve the outcome you desire, no matter how easy or difficult the task.

In the "eye of a storm," there is always a light that won't go out, a friend that will ensure you are never alone, and a place you can retreat to and have no fear. There is a way to find courage to endure whatever comes your way. To have all these available is easy and takes about twenty seconds. Simply take a knee and ask.

There are only two things in life that are stronger than anything in the world, natural or manmade. They are also the two things that are the most fragile and can be totally shattered: a person's heart and their faith! Be it heart or faith, their strength depends upon only one thing, the person they belong to, for neither can be broken or shattered, stolen, or taken away unless you allow it!

Everyone has a fear of something. To relate that fear to another can be a fear in itself for many reasons. To do so may expose the vulnerability you have, which no one, especially a warrior, would desire to do. However, to do so may also make you stronger as your fear is confronted and perhaps even dispelled once it is not kept bottled up and got out in the open to deal with.

It is neat to see what one is capable of, whether one is handicapped or not, when they try to push themselves beyond their current physical limitations. It is totally amazing to see how far those limits can be exceeded when one adds all the strength and commitment of their heart behind pushing their physical limits! When the body says I have given my all, the committed heart behind it will find a way to make one take another step, extend one's reach one more inch, do one more repetition, endure the elements just a little longer, or hang on just a few more seconds.

Reality is something you can see, taste, touch, smell, or believe in, without compromising what you believe to be morally right or wrong. It is also not turning a "blind eye" to what is going on around you, that which is ugly, wrong, corrupt, and places no value on life. Reality is being willing to stand up for what you believe in and get your hands dirty trying to "take out the trash" of anything that litters the "gardens of beauty" in your life. It sucks, but there are only two choices: remove the litter or allow your corner of the world to become a garbage dump. If you chose the latter . . . enjoy your rubbish and don't complain about it!

You will never realize how high you can climb, if part of you is always scared of how far you might fall!

Often in life, it is not as important to have an answer to our problems as it is to understand the problem itself.

Life can indeed be a dance. It can be reflective of a soft, tender hold you close and take your breath away slow dance that seems to suspend time for one beautiful moment. Other times, life can be as upbeat to dance to as a number one song on a "Pop Music Chart." Life can also be as sad as the soft shuffle to a ballad or folk tune reminiscing of better times or the lost love of one's past. No doubt about it, with busy work schedules, kids schedules to juggle, and the fast pace of the "Gotta have it now" technology age, life is most often reflective of the dancing in a "mosh pit" at a "Heavy Metal" concert. I personally believe everyone would benefit from trying to add the time to dance to a few more "slow songs" in their life.

Tears are the nourishing rains that provide nutrients to the soil in your soul and allow a very good harvest of "character" to grow. Without experiencing something in your life that would cause enough of an emotion to "let it rain," your character could not be forged by the "blacksmith of life" with the temper it needs to have to make it strong!

Above all else, always be true to yourself!

Life plays a tune that everyone can dance to. What is important isn't how we'll you dance, or what dance you do. What is important is that you dance!

The secret to happiness isn't a secret. It has been revealed thousands of times in various ways by multitudes who are very ordinary people . . . no special powers . . . no crystal balls . . . no special potions . . . just ordinary people, who simply realize this: it's not personal wealth, titles, who you know, or where you live that matters. It is not your IQ score, your level of education, your physical shape, or your religion that matters. It is simply being able to love yourself for who you are and then sharing that love with others, in the form of a smile, kind word, or kind deed.

A promise is only a promise if the spoken words are followed through to fulfillment as voluntarily stated. If they are not, or if actions and deeds fall short of the words which preceded them, the promise becomes nothing more than a lie, no matter how you paint it. Say what you mean, mean what you say, and let honor being associated with your name be the outcome.

A positive attitude is half of the solution to addressing many problems. Keeping an open mind and being an active listener is another 40 percent, leaving a problem that is a manageable 10 percent in size versus the monster it was before attacking it with your armor of attitude and weapons of problem solving and positive communication skills.

If you can manage to smile at danger, laugh at adversity, and wink at controversy even though you may not feel like it on the inside, it may just be enough to give you a better perspective from which to analyze your problem and come up with a plausible solution.

To forgive when possible is to free one of the bonds and excess baggage that could prevent you from enjoying life and moving at a quicker pace to a more wonderful place. To forget would be foolish, as it will keep you from traveling down the roads that are not worth sightseeing on.

Everyone has freedom. There are internal and external freedoms, and not everyone has been blessed to have both. One can be restricted, regulated, and even taken away. The other, no one can take, steal, limit, or govern. However, you can choose to give it up . . . and hope along with it. They both have a common denominator . . . someone paid a price for them. To them, we all owe a debt. To pay it off is to pay it forward by preserving it for those who will follow us. This can only be done with actions, words, and by example. To be a quiet passive, voice is but a step in giving away the most precious of gifts one could ever have or pass on to another.

Sometimes, the very hardest thing to do during the day is to convince yourself that it is okay to just sit down, kick your feet up, and do absolutely nothing but enjoy a few minutes for you!

Live your life as though for a camera. It does not mean you must try to get a perfect pose or the perfect photo. It rather means if someone snapped a photo of you at any given moment and posted it all over the Internet, you would not have any reason to be embarrassed or ashamed!

To a soldier, the fight is always for those we love. It is not about those we hate.

Almost everything today has an original version and a generic one. You can get something full or half-strength, something like the real thing, but not. A product, that works almost as well as, is very similar too, and hard to tell the difference between, the real thing and the imitation item. For marketing and manufactured goods, replicas and spin-offs of the original are fine. However, for character, there is only one version acceptable. The original honesty in word and deed and in all of your actions and dealings with others version! Character; have it, demand it, and accept no substitute!

The only thing we can't start over again in life is our birth. Other than that, it's never too late to start something over again . . . to start new habits (let go of bad ones), right a wrong, mend a friendship or relationship, change a career, change a lifestyle, your environment, and your attitude, or change your mind. Life is all about change. Don't be afraid to give it a try.

Being an optimist and always striving to have a positive attitude by no means guarantees you will never have sad, depressing, or downright "crappy" days. Everyone on the planet has them. The difference is when they come around, you try to paint on a smile and make the best of them! That alone can almost cut the impact of those days in half, when one does happen to land in your lap.

When it comes right down to it, no one can dictate our happiness . . . no one, not even God, or we would not have free agency over ourselves. Although through him, we can find it. However, it is often hard to remember that and make use of that knowledge when we let others get too deep into our hearts who end up hurting and being reckless with them. Remember, for someone to be able to hurt your heart, they must have done something wonderful or the loss would not matter. Focus on that, and remember, there is always someone else with the potential to fill the void if you are willing to let them.

Remember, no matter how tough the path is that you are traveling, the creator of all of life's pathways ensured they were all wide enough that, if you wanted, you could travel them with a dear friend at your side.

Life is fragile, yet we run rough shod through it with little regard for its fragility. Life is hard, yet we opt to hit potholes in the road our self and not follow detour signs of others who have hit the hole before us.

I think two of the most important words in language, any language, that seem to me to have lost their importance to society in general is "loyal" and "faithful." According to Webster's Dictionary, as a synonym, faithful is a steadfast adherence to a person or thing; and a definition of loyalty is a faithful adherence to a person, government, cause, or duty . . . It is said "if you don't stand for something, you'll die for nothing" (unknown). If we would be loyal and faithful in our actions, words, and deeds, with the unwavering determination of our nation's "founding fathers," everyday would be a day we could hold our heads high knowing our actions, words, and deeds were backed by a solid foundation of goodness that could not be challenged, questioned, reputed, or anything else but admired! Just my opinion . . .

It has been said, and we all know, that all of us have a thousand different wishes. Some wish to lose weight and be thinner. Yet others wish to gain weight and be more muscular. We wish we had more money, better jobs, cool cars, the latest smartphones, and tablets. Some wish to date and marry the person of their dreams. We wish for longer vacations, cruises, and trips to exotic tropical islands . . . bigger houses, televisions, jewelry, and the latest fashion designer clothes. A cancer patient has but one wish: to kick cancer's ass! Those who lose someone they treasure, a loved one, or a dear friend to cancer, wish for just one more day with that loved one or dear friend that they lost. I hope I see the day we find a cure for cancer. Until then, prioritize your wishes now, as one day material things will have little value to you!

Kindness . . . If we don't teach our children, it is a lesson of importance that the world will not teach them!

Life is not like a Las Vegas poker game. People will not respect you and give you "high-five's," if you pull a good "bluff" over on them. In fact, it's not even called "bluffing" in real life. It is called lying!

We know we reap what we sow, yet, for some reason, we run around planting briar patches and thistles rather than orchids. That is, until tragedy strikes, then we want to pay attention, unite, help one another, and call upon God for help . . . and we unite, and we care, and we help one another, and we witness prayers answered. And then time passes, and we unlock arms, we forget about God, we say "screw the neighbor," yell the homeless to get a job, and are back in the fast lane of life, planting thistles! That is until the next tragedy strikes. Let us all have longer memories, embrace one another a little longer, watch for detour signs, smile, help a stranger, slow down, and thank God in hope that through remembering, we all might choose to plant a few more orchids than thistles.

Thoughts, ideas, and dreams are not meant to be something we should enjoy once and file away. Rather they are to be used like our own internal GPS system, meant to guide us down paths and roads to resources along the way that can help us achieve and make our dreams come true.

As I see it, there are but two ways to tackle problems: "sleeves or sand!" The "sleeve theory," being that you look at your problem, roll up your sleeves, be the aggressor, and not be afraid, get dirty doing or sacrificing as you hit the problem head on until the problem is solved, defeated, eliminated, or beat down to a manageable load to bear . . . or the "sand theory," in which you simply just stick your head in the sand like an ostrich and pretend, by not seeing or hearing it, that it will magically just go away if you ignore it long enough. This theory, of course, never works! Revert to "sleeve theory." I already know someone will say that there is a third option: turn the problem over to God. God helps those who help themselves, or that at least put forth a good effort on their own first before opting for divine intervention. Therefore, if you want to solicit his helping hand, refer back to the "sleeve theory" and get a blister or two on your hands before bending your knees! That is according to the "Blue Collar Philosopher" anyway (me).

Everyone can make a difference in someone else's life. You don't have to be good with words, you don't have to know fifteen different languages, and you don't have to have a PhD or be a doctor of anything, or hold any political office either. All one has to do is care, share a smile with someone when you have the opportunity, and never be in too big of a hurry to listen to someone who is trusting you to hear what they have to say.

Not everyone is looking for a handout. Some just simply need a "hand-up!"

Everything that comes out of our mouth is like a knife! With our words, the knife can be used on its side to spread things around gently, like butter on toast. Or our words can come out like a knife held straight up and down in a manner to stab, poke, or, with the right motion, slice. These types of words hurt people, some badly. Over words, friendships have ended and wars have stared . . . choose your words carefully and spread love . . . words that cause hurt can stick with someone for a lifetime.

Sometimes when the world around us is total chaos and we need a small reprieve, there is a place within all of us where we can find a bit of peace . . . when time allows, all we need to do to access it is to take a bended knee.

If I could have anything in the world for a birthday wish . . . it would simply be a totally smiling stress-free day for every single one of my awesome Facebook friends!

Everyone has a story, and I have yet to meet or hear of anyone whose book is titled "My Totally Wonderful Life, Without Any Pain, Hurt, Sickness, Heartache, Depression, Disease, or Tragedy." So before you judge someone, remember that they may just be trying their very hardest to survive just one single day at a time to get through the very worst chapter in their book of life, not gloating over an ending that says, "And they lived happily ever after!"

The difference between a gold and silver medal, first place and second place, winning and losing, isn't determined by centimeters, or seconds and milliseconds, in yards, by car lengths, or even on a scoreboard. No, I believe it is measured, no matter the event, sports, war, or business, in but two places: the heart and mind of those who are fighting to come out as winners. Determination and will power make the difference! Those who want it bad enough train harder and longer and push themselves further on and off the field of battle. When the time comes to perform, their only competition is themselves, for the fear of losing is bigger, stronger, and faster than any other opponent they will ever face!

Dare to be different! Dare to do a random act of kindness. Dare to be the one to smile first at someone. Dare to acknowledge that a majority of the world has it worse off than you and go a whole day without complaining. Dare to give someone a complement, and dare to give yourself one too. The difference it will make just might surprise the hell right out of you!

If you find you have a hard time saying kind things about others or giving someone a compliment, you probably have just as hard of a time saying something good and positive and uplifting about yourself. Make an effort, a serious effort, to start your day off, every single morning, by complimenting the awesome person you see looking back at you in the mirror each morning. You'll be surprised at the smile it will put on your face and the ripple effect it will have on others too!

Everything needs cleaning from time to time. For tough stains on clothes, we can directly spray a stain remover on the stain before washing. Hearts are a little different, since we can't apply a stain remover directly on them; that is why we have tears! Tears are a stain remover for the heart, and a good cry from time to time is just washing it.

The way anyone acts, looks, dresses, or treats people and animals on their best day tells you little about them. It is how we can act, react, and interact with others on our worst of days, which we learn and gain insight into one's true character. The one common denominator is with honest eye's, we can all see and find ways to improve!

September 11, 2001: We said we would never forget! Let us all have a moment to remember, in reverence, those who died on this fateful day as well as those who have fallen since and those still fighting to protect and preserve all we cherish . . . our country, freedom, liberty, opportunity, family . . . love! Let us all *never forget!*

Chasing your dreams requires not only ambition, drive, and hard work, but faith as well. For when you are shooting for the stars, you can't quit when the sun comes out just because you cannot see them! You must totally have unwavering faith that the stars are still there so that you can maintain your momentum until you can actually see them again!

There is nothing wrong with having a different opinion than someone else. Wouldn't it suck if every car on your morning commute was the same make, model, and color and all playing the exact same one song on the radio all the way to work . . . where everyone dressed the exact same! Unless it is immoral, illegal, or infringes on the rights of another, have tolerance, because it is the ability to express different opinions that make us unique, add variety to our lives, and give us the momentum to chase dreams.

If you say it, mean it. If you mean it, follow through on it, and make it happen! It gets old having people tell you anything they think you want to hear just to get you off the phone, out of their office, or out of their way. Customer service and people who keep their word are few and far between anymore!

Perfection is something never to be obtained for good reason. There is always room for improvement . . . always something new to reach for just outside your grasp. If you were truly perfect, what would be the use of living if there were no longer mountains for you to aspire to reach the summit of? Don't seek to be perfect . . . you'll find nothing but constant disappointments. Rather always try to do your best, and always reach just a little further than your grasp!

Faith, no matter how big a house, mansion, or castle you live in, will never take up more room than the size of your heart.

"One good thing about music, when it hits you, you feel no pain."—Bob Marley . . . So true! The power of music can totally change your mood, within hearing just a few notes or chords of a song that has deep meaning to you!

"Perfection" is one word I have a dislike for in any language! It is unobtainable in the world in which we live. This may cause many to give up on challenges or self-improvement they are striving for by trying to be perfect! Instead say, "I will make a conscious effort to be a better person today than I was yesterday!" If you truly make an honest attempt to be a better you every day, the transformation you will feel, you will see, and the effect that positive energy will have on others is endless. Trying to constantly make self-improvements is better than perfection, which alludes to an ending point because it is finite, and there is nothing that, as time will reveal, cannot be improved upon!

I do not think God or any other "higher power" you believe in will give you all the answers to every question you ask or personally guide you down every single path you travel in life. I do believe that through faith, you can be spiritually led to a place or someone who can help you find answers or receive an affirmation in your heart that you are thinking correctly and on the right path. God wants us to be problem solvers and make our own decisions; hence, "free agency!" Rely on your faith for guidance and trust in yourself to make decisions on some of the hard choices that need to be made while navigating down life's highway!

No, you won't always make the right choice the first time! If we were meant to always be right, words like "sorry," "forgiveness," "repentance," and "restitution" would not exist!

There is always decision to be made in our every action, and it is not always "is it right or wrong?" Sometimes, the decision is simply "should I do it?" That is where ambition and often courage come into play. Don't pass up an opportunity for yourself or to perhaps help someone else simply because you are afraid to act! Sometimes, a bad decision is better than not making any decision at all!

True peace is found when your heart and mind agree to accept what is unknown and find the beauty in a balance of nature, mankind, and the universe which surrounds us. That does not mean not to seek answers; just enjoy the treasure hunt and do not get discouraged if you don't always find what you are looking for.

Dear President George Washington, as the celebrated "father of our country," I am sad to say that I do not believe you would be pleased at all with how well we have taken care of the freedom, the liberties, and the country you fought so bravely for us to live in today. However, there are still patriots among us, also brave and true, willing to fight for what is right, just like you. We will band together and, just like you would desire, ensure that what you created does not get tossed recklessly into the fire.

I like the acronym K.I.S.S. (keep it simple stupid). I like things black and white, right and wrong, and don't believe in shades of gray. Something is simply the truth or a lie. There are no half-truths! That would still be a lie. Things are not half-bad. That still makes them not all good. People are no different. You can have good friends or bad. There are no half-good ones. If you want good friends, be one; expect the same in return! After all, you wouldn't hire a contractor to build you a house and then leave without putting a roof on it. That is just doing "half the job!" Why accept less anywhere else in your life?

What is it that is so easy that currently less than 20 percent of the eligible population is doing in some areas of the country? Simply this . . . *vote!* Stay informed and cast an educated vote on everything that is put on a ballot in your voting precinct for the entire year. If everyone let their voice be heard, collectively, more sound decisions would be made by the government we have let become reckless with the domestic, foreign, and fiscal policies that affect us.

Often when you miss a club or organization meeting you belong to that you usually never miss, or are absent from work which is out of character for you; or if you are not seen at a local hangout you normally stop at after work or on a weekend, you can almost count on a knock on your door that same day or hearing a phone that doesn't receive a lot of calls "ringing off the hook." Who will it be? They are simply called your "dear" or "best friends!"

Gone are the days a handshake and one's word were an unbreakable bond that were more secure than anything written or signed on any piece of paper. Why? Because personal character, dignity, and the protecting of one's family name from being associated with anything that is not honest and just lack the importance as a society we once prioritized. The moral decline in our society is eroding and breaking the threads that hold the great "tapestry of Americana" together. Keep your thread strong by being honest in your dealings with others and by not being afraid to stand up for what you believe is right! Regardless whether your position is popular, if you believe it to be right, stand your ground.

Because you answered the call, when Lady Liberty needed you, our sovereignty has been preserved. Because you gave your all when our country needed you to, our freedoms have been protected and preserved. Because you stood tall with courage when the fires of hell and stench of death consumed you, I did not have to live in fear and could chase my dreams. Because of your honor, heroes were forged, and teachers and mentors came forward to teach me that freedom does not come without a heavy price. You taught me how to respect that and show respect for those who have fought for it and died for it. Through your example, I learned to love and respect the flag that represents all we believe in as a nation, our flag. Because of your example, I knew I had a duty to take my turn to carry and pass along safely the torch of freedom that you kept burning so bright on your watch! On this day dear veterans, this Veterans Day, I humbly thank and salute you all . . . Thank you!

Why is it that those who complain the most about roads live in a place where there is not a pothole anywhere And those who never complain about sidewalks, nice jogging, biking paths, and walkways do not have any even available? Those who complain loudest about public transportation never use it, or even carpool for that matter. Complaints about public schools come from those who never attend a parent-teacher conference or volunteer to assist teachers in their children's classrooms or help chaperone on field trips. Those who complain most about income taxes pay very little of them and seldom vote, or realize the heavy burden they are under with sales tax, and additional fuel taxes. It is sad to know most citizens do not even know legislators are in session at state and national levels, have an interest in, or care to find out what is being introduced on house and senate floors that could have a huge impact on them. It is even sadder to know that most people do not even know who their representative is to call and voice an opinion to, if they even had one. There is no point to any of this . . . just venting.

Nothing can warm your heart faster or put things in their proper perspective as fast as a smile from a small child or laughter shared with a dear friend.

To have a true friend, you must be one. Therefore, you should both know how to tread water, because the ship will "go under" while true friends are both arguing over trying to get the other to take the last available seat in the life boat!

Blown up six times in that hell hole Iraq, determined and focused he finally made it back. Now his mission is patriotism, inspiration and love, with a passionate force coming only from above. His service to our country deserves endless attention, his sacrifices and suffering too numerous to mention. Who is this soldier as tough as a mule? Why of course, he is none other than Gordon L. Ewell.

—Louis Hall
Southern Belle
Florence, KY

This is my dear friend Louis Hall, as sweet and charitable a woman as you could ever meet!
(02-01-2013).

Freedom Isn't Free
(Photo by Melanie Toll Schramm owner of
Melanie's Photo Shoppe Photography)

After being severely wounded during the war in Iraq in 2006, I began a new journey on what would be a very long road to recovery. One war ended for me, and another began, my war after the war, learning to survive in a world with the severe handicaps I have. This war I will fight for the rest of my life.

I have had major cranial facial reconstructive surgeries. I broke the sixth vertebra in my neck, which healed wrong, causing some right-side stenosis (restricted blood flow to my brain), which is probably the cause of my left-side neglect (My brain does not often recognize the world on my left side.).

I am legally blind. I have had my right eye removed. While I do not have any bilateral fields of vision in my left eye and only see an area about the size of a paper plate at any one time, I still have a small amount of useable vision in my left eye, for which I am very thankful.

I realize a totally blind person would give anything to be able to have the sight I have.

I am legally deaf, although I can hear a limited amount via a hearing aid in my right ear. I have received a cochlear implant in my inner left ear, and I am hopeful and optimistic that one day I may be able to hear some sounds in stereo again.

Although I am legally deaf, I still have some ability to hear. I realize a totally deaf person would give anything to be able to have the limited ability to hear that I have.

I have an abnormal gait. I require the use of a "blind-man" cane and a support cane to get around. Sometimes, I need a walker, a wheelchair, and/or an assistant to get around. But for the most part, I can get around with the use of an aid of some kind on my own feet.

I realize that someone who is totally restricted to a wheelchair or who is paralyzed would give anything to have my mobility problems.

While I have been on a liquid or soft diet for the better part of five years, I realize that someone with a feeding tube would give anything to be able to be on my diet.

I have some memory problems. I suffer from severe PTSD. Someone with Alzheimer's disease would give anything to be able to remember things . . . even nightmares or traumatic events I imagine.

I guess all I am trying to point out is that no matter how bad off things are for each of us, no matter what our trials or how heavy the burdens are that we shoulder, there is always someone who has it worse off than we do and would joyfully swap their troubles for ours.

Knowing this does not make our burdens lighter, it does not make pain hurt less, and it does not make financial worries disappear, what I believe it can do, however, or how I use this knowledge, is from the standpoint of perspective. By reminding myself it could be worse, I find strength to endure while I put up a fight. By changing my perspective of how I look at my problems, I have found that I have also been able to find new ways to deal with them . . . positive ways. I have found that just being able to have a more positive outlook on my situation can indeed make me feel better and often see a different way of doing things that can make the way I deal with my handicaps and burdens a lot easier.

Thinking of just one positive thought or one thing to be grateful for each day and reminding myself of that one thing throughout the day, when things start to feel overwhelming to me, often helps to hold off a bout with the depression monster that usually stops by my place every day wanting to come inside and play.

My "Gordy-isms" are that one thought each day for me. It is just another tool for my toolbox, along with many others, to help me get through each day.

I do believe a positive attitude, smiles, and laughter have a healing power. They certainly are not a cure-all, but they surely help.

I hope you found some of my "Gordy-isms" did just that and made you smile, laugh, and for a moment, no matter how brief, took your mind off your own troubles or worries.

Better still, I hope that perhaps they have inspired you to think of your own positive "isms" each day to ponder on and find joy in.

I hope then that perhaps one day, you will share your positive thoughts, your own "isms," with me.

I believe that every day, there is inherent in something or someone that will cross our path that will have the ability to make our day a little brighter, if we just look for it.

I also believe that every day someone will cross our path that is in need of a "pick-me-up," a smile, a laugh, or even a helping hand. Hopefully, we will all be aware of this, and not let someone who is hurting pass us by, without us being the smile or laugh they needed, to help get them through their day.

No one sails through their time on this spinning orb we call Earth, or home, solo! At some time or another, we all need a helping hand. If we all remembered that and were always looking to be that helping hand for someone in need, what a totally different life experience we would have. Just think what a better world it would be to live in if everyone was always looking for an opportunity to do good for another.

We definitely cannot change the world. However, collectively, we all have the potential to change our little corner of it for the better!

Remember, when in doubt, smile!

Friend me on Facebook to read the "Gordy-isms" I continue to post regularly: Gordon Ewell from Eagle Mountain, UT: http://www. facebook.com/gordy0406

You can also find me at www.dunginmyfoxhole.com. This is my personal webpage, showing upcoming events I will be at, the books I have published, photo galleries, TV and radio interviews, and many valuable resources where wounded warriors, veterans, and their families can get aid and assistance or just find answers to questions they may have. Hope to see you there!

www.blustarriders.com dedicated to assisting hospitalized wounded warriors and veterans.

Or contact me by e-mail at gordyewell@yahoo.com

Speaking and book signing in Billings, MT
(07-20-2013).

Speaking to elementary school children

In the end, it is not what you can do for yourself. It is about what you can do for others and what you can pass along to today to ensure all a better tomorrow.

Answering some questions with some of the student body after speaking at a school assembly on patriotism and citizenship

During an assembly speaking to Junior High School Students about freedom
(Kevin White (L) and Kam Wright (R)

Author Gordon L Ewell
(10-04-2013)
(Photo by Melanie Toll Schramm owner of Melanie's
Photo Shoppe Photography)

"People are often unreasonable and self-centered. Forgive them anyway.

If you are kind, people may cheat you. Be honest anyway.

If you find happiness, people may be jealous. Be happy anyway.

The good you do today may be forgotten tomorrow. Do good anyway.

Give the world the best you have and it may never be enough. Give your best anyway.

For you see, in the end, it is between you and God. It was never between you and them anyway.

—Mother Teresa

Gordon L. Ewell
During a book signing event
(2013)

About the Author

Master Sergeant (MSG) Gordon L. Ewell was born on June 8, 1967, and graduated from Emery County High School in May 1985. He joined the Utah Army National Guard on August 28, 1985, with initial assignment to the 1457th Engineer Battalion as a combat engineer. In August 1991, he transitioned to the Active Guard Reserve program, with Delta Company, of the 1457th Engineer Battalion.

His twenty-four-year career has been marked with distinction through notable accomplishments that render him an excellent example for other soldiers to follow.

Throughout his outstanding military career, he has served in key positions as training and administration specialist, supply sergeant, combat engineer squad leader, and personnel section sergeant.

From MSG Gordon L Ewell's initial entry into Military Service, his superiors recognized his outstanding initiative and a deep care for his fellow soldiers. He has been recognized as one who would do whatever it takes to accomplish the mission or help a fellow soldier in need. His twenty-four-year career has been marked with distinction through notable accomplishments. MSG Ewell has graduated from over thirty Army Resident Schools, graduating as the honor graduate, or in the top 10 percent of his class, from nearly every one of them.

He has completed, with a "superior" rating, over 1,000 hours of Army Correspondence Training. Additionally, he earned an Associate of Science degree in April 1999.

During his service in Iraq, MSG Ewell performed fifty-nine challenging and dangerous missions, which involved both the coordination of Convoy Route Clearance and Route Clearance Observation missions, based upon his knowledge and expertise in these areas. MSG Ewell was vital in the creation of the first Route Clearance Handbook and was further recognized by the Corps staff as the Multi-National Corps "Subject Matter Expert," in Route Clearance. His lessons learned in Iraq have been published in many Army periodicals.

MSG Ewell led over 33 percent of the missions he was on in Iraq. He was recognized by his superiors to be unparalleled in his physical stamina and toughness complemented with superior technical and tactical capabilities. This was clearly demonstrated on the battlefield when his efforts under heavy enemy fire were unrivaled, which earned him a Bronze Star Medal, the Purple Heart Medal, and the Combat Action Badge.

During his combat missions, on six separate occasions, a vehicle he was in was blown up by improvised explosive devices (IEDs). One of the explosions was so powerful that it blew impacted wisdom teeth out the side of his jaw. In addition to major jaw damage, he suffers from broken vertebrae in his neck, damage to his lower spine, and permanent loss of hearing (leaving him legally deaf).

He suffered the anatomical loss of his right eye and peripheral/bilateral vision loss in his left eye, leaving him legally blind. He has a traumatic brain injury (TBI), flaccid neurologic bladder, loss of balance, an abnormal gait, and is fighting to overcome Post-Traumatic Stress Disorder (PTSD).

MSG Ewell returned from combat duty in December 2006 and was assigned to the 640th Regiment (Regional Training Institute). Because of the severity of his combat injuries, he was medically retired from injuries sustained while at war in February 2010.

His "medical journey" to date has included six major surgeries, treatment at eight different hospitals, in three states, by over forty-seven different doctors, surgeons, specialists, and other health care professionals; like more than a dozen different dentists, endodontists, oral surgeons, and mental health professionals.

Today, though he is 100 percent disabled, he continues to serve with distinction, as a vice president of the Blue Star Riders, as a volunteer at the George E. Wahlen V.A. Hospital in Salt Lake City, with the Veterans of Foreign Wars, Disabled American Veterans, American Legion, and the Military Order of the Purple Heart.

He constantly travels the county, doing motivational, patriotic speaking, and sharing his story with veterans and veteran organizations, public and private schools, Rotary clubs, Chambers of Commerce, at colleges and universities, and political functions, basically, anywhere and to anyone who wants to be inspired!

He is very passionate and enjoys public peaking, writing, helping other veterans, and the beach.

He loves attempting anything someone tells him that he cannot do: fixing and building things, and wood working.

One last love of his is watching the sunrise, and the sunset, on the deck of his home while enjoying the peace, beauty, and serenity, with a good cup of coffee and enjoying it even more if a friend comes over for a visit to enjoy it with him.

The retired master sergeant currently resides in Eagle Mountain, Utah. He enjoys, above all, being a father and watching his two beautiful little princesses grow, learn, and excel in school, and every second he gets to play with them. He is grounded and committed to his family, extended family, and his friends and would fly to their aid, without question, if ever they needed him!

My *beautiful princesses:*
Scarlett (left) and Lincoln (right)
They are the center of my life!
(02-06-2013).

University of Utah Veterans Day Ceremony
One of eleven veterans honored at the Veterans Day
ceremony, and the first Post-Vietnam Era Veteran to ever
be commemorated at the annual inductee ceremony.

In my Army dress uniform
(08-18-2013)
(Photo courtesy of Melanie Schramm, Melanie's
Photo Shoppe Photography)

MILITARY AWARDS AND DECORATIONS

Bronze Star Medal
Purple Heart Medal
Meritorious Service Medal
Army Commendation Medal (with Bronze Oak Leaf)
Army Achievement Medal
Army Good Conduct Medal (with six Bronze Knots)
Army Reserve Components Achievement Medal (with three Bronze Oak Leafs)
National Defense Service Medal (with Bronze Star)
Iraq Campaign Medal (with Campaign Star)
Global War on Terrorism Service Medal
Armed Forces Reserve Medal (with "M" Devise and Silver Hourglass)
NCO Professional Development Ribbon (3rd Award)
Army Service Ribbon
Overseas Service Ribbon
Army Reserve Components Overseas Training Ribbon (3rd Award)
Combat Action Badge
Diver and Mechanic Badge (with wheeled vehicle clasp)
Sharpshooter Weapon Marksmanship Badge
Utah Commendation Medal (3rd award)
Utah 2002 Olympic Winter Games Service Ribbon
Utah Emergency Service Ribbon
Utah Achievement Ribbon
Utah Recruiting Ribbon
Utah Service Ribbon

Joint Meritorious Unit Award
Army Superior Unit Award

Noteworthy Civilian Achievements

On November 9, 2012, the University of Utah held its fourteenth Annual Veterans Day Ceremony, presenting honorary medallions to eleven veterans from four different wars. I was honored to be among the eleven selected and the first veteran honored since Vietnam

Presented the key to the city of Leitchfield, Kentucky, by Honorable Mayor William H. Thomason on August 12, 2012

Commissioned as a Kentucky Colonel by the honorable governor, Steven L. Beshear, and the honorable secretary of State Alison Lundergan Grimes, of the Commonwealth of Kentucky, August 10, 2012 (the 221st year of the Commonwealth)

Made an Honorable Duke of the city of Paducha, Kentucky, by Honorable Mayor Hardy Gentry on August 10, 2012

Honored to be made an Honorary Member of Rotary International, with membership in the Park City, Utah Sunrise Club (August 15, 2011)

Elected as the senior vice commander of his Disabled American Veterans Section, Wasatch One, Utah (August 3, 2011)

Selected as vice president of the Blue Star Riders, honoring and helping our nation's hospitalized soldiers and their families (September 2010)

Was one of six people from Utah selected to hand-stitch the Utah section onto the National 9/11 Flag that now resides at the museum at Ground Zero as a National Memorial and Treasure (July 2011)

Received The State of Utah Department of Public Safety Executive Award of Merit, in recognition and appreciation of extraordinary service and outstanding contributions on behalf of the citizens of Utah (2008)

Presented City of Eagle Mountain Outstanding Citizenship Award (2007)

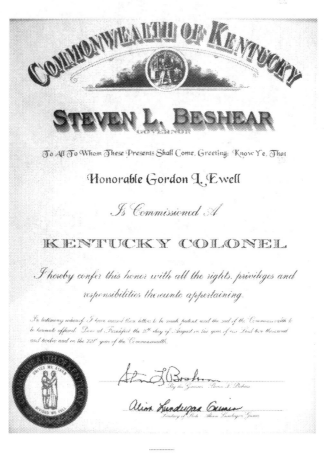

I am proud to have been a "Defender of Freedom!"
(08-18-2013)
(Photo courtesy of Melanie Schramm, Melanie's Photo
Shoppe Photography. Thank you my dear friend!)

ACKNOWLEDGMENTS

I was, in a nutshell, a bomb hunter during the war in Iraq in 2006 at a time when incidents with improvised explosive devices (IEDs) or "roadside bombs," were peaking at over 3,100 a month, over one hundred a day, every day! An incident being either a bomb we found, or one that found us. I was in a vehicle that was blown up literally six different times by a roadside bomb within ten feet of the vehicle and a seventh time by a mortar round that landed next to the vehicle I was in. In essence, I feel I cheated death seven times. It is a very small, little family, those with the mission of route clearance. I lost several "brothers" I had forged good friendships with, "brothers" who one single bomb made them a memory to me. It was hard then. It remains so today. I was very severely wounded. I suffered a very long and painful recovery, and I am still suffering. However, I am alive. My friends are not. I count each day as a blessing. That being said, I feel everyone in my life is a blessing . . . literally! I feel like I need to acknowledge everyone who has made an impact on my life and everyone who is in my life today! Let me rephrase that. Because I do feel so blessed by everyone in my life, I *want* to list by name and acknowledge *everyone* who is in my life. There is truly *none* of you who I am not thankful for in my life or who I do not feel has been the inspiration for a positive thought or "Gordy-ism" that has helped me along my recovery road. To do so, however, would take more pages than there are in this book. The thought of this alone makes me feel very humbled and feel very blessed. For this warmth in my heart, I thank you all.

Heartfelt thanks to Facebook friends who inspire and encourage me to keep posting "Gordy-isms" regularly.

Continued thanks to my family in the bluegrass of Kentucky, whose love and support is nothing short of inspiring: Jim and April Lish, Pete and Janett Galauner, Lois Hall, Dick Heaton, Misty Embry Thomas, Dr. Pete Trzop, John Barton, Joan Deyo, Anthony Noe, Carol Duke, Robert Bryant, Larry Crabbtree, Scott Dalton, Mayor Hardy Gentry, Ron Stiers, Mayor William Thomason, Mike and Sharon Roberts, Mike and Heather Bowman and Scotty Frank.

Stacy Bare and P.W. Covington, for always advocating for our veterans, I am honored to be your brother.

To new friends and family in Montana, for unwavering patriotism: Merv Gunderson (American Legion National Executive Committee Member for Montana), Andrew Pearson Post #117; The Northern Hotel in Billings, MT, George Blackard and family, Luke Walker and Family; Bill and Dawn Hoefer, Steve and Kari Longshore, Elizabeth Fletcher, "TJ" Smith, Ryan Harper, and Larry McGovern (an awesome volunteer).

Thank you, to the Squire Lounge in Billings, Montana; dear friends Jeff and JoLynne Flatness, and Pauly.

To my brother, Mitch Howe, there are not enough words, but there is enough silence, to sit on your porch together and visit for hours without saying a thing.

Thanks to the Chance Phelps Foundation, and Jeff and Gretchen Mack, much love, and to Alan Truesdale too.

Thanks to friends, employees, and volunteers at VA Hospitals in Salt Lake City, Utah, and Palo Alto, CA.

John Gonsalvez leads the fight for wounded veterans. See his webpage at www.SAHmission.org Thanks John.

Thanks Van Curaza, surf instructor, for sharing the healing power of the ocean (Amazing Surf Adventures).

Thanks to Nola Pedersen Mikich for endless kindness.

Much love to Stacy Snow and Cindy Funk—true friends that are a constant source of encouragement.

Thank you to my friend Montel Williams, for his example of never giving up when battling illness or disability. I am humbled by all you have done for me.

Thank-you to Ann Jensen for a family friendship that reflects unconditional love (Christmas time will never be the same or without tons of laughs).

Aunt Marilynn, I love you (Merrell and Alan too). I don't know where your halo is, but know you have one.

To Jeff Sagers, your friendship is "solid as a rock!"

Special thanks to my brother Jerry Bishop and to Todd Christensen for special lunches; each one is a treasure!

Thank you to John Glines for his friendship and always letting me ride to the east with him.

My friend Paul Swenson's Patriotic Heart inspires me!

To my dear friends Dell and Connie Smith, you have continued to ensure that I have been able to participate in functions and activities that are important to me, that I would not be able to attend if it were not for you. I remain so very grateful and humbled to be your friend.

To my best friend Richard Hamilton, I love you brother. A man could not find anyone who would never stop giving more than you "Wolf (Marsha too)!

Thank you, Jack Nitz, my friend, you are a giant among men! Thank you for the mobility you have given me and so many others through your Eagle Cane Project!

Mom and Dad . . . you have continued to show me what unconditional love is! Literally no matter what time, day or night, no matter the trouble or circumstance, no matter the cost, financially or of your time, energy, or to your heart, you are always there for me! I love you both will all my heart!

Rod and Marjory Ewell
My Mom and Dad
(2013)

I could not have a brother or sisters who are loved more than I love mine. They are all examples and sources of strength to me, as are their beautiful families!

To my little princesses, Scarlett Olivia and Lincoln Abbygale, Daddy loves you more than you could ever know. You were too small when Daddy got hurt to know much about or have a memory of how badly Daddy got hurt. But you two angels are the reasons Daddy never gave up and never stopped fighting to get better; you are the reasons Daddy will always keep fighting so that I will always be able to love and care for you, and play with you, protect you, and provide for you also. You two will always be the most special treasure that I keep in my heart! You will always be the brightest stars in my night sky. Never a day will pass that there are not kisses blown into the wind for both of you. One of these days, you will be able to teach me how to do a cartwheel without falling! I love you to the moon and back and always will!

My Beautiful Princesses
Miss Scarlett Olivia (L) and Miss Lincoln Abbygale (R).

Daddy's Girls
With my awesome princesses Scarlett and Lincoln
(08-02-2013)

Governor Gary Herbert (UT)

Above: Proud to call Utah Governor Gary Herbert and
Below: Congressman Matheson and Senator Lee friends!
I am grateful for all they do for our veterans!

Congressman Jim Matheson (UT) Senator Mike Lee (UT)

Me and Randy Jones at Mount Rushmore
With dear friend Randy Jones at Sturgis Rally (2013).

The "boys" at Bristol, NASCAR all the way! (2013)
Someone said they seen Jim Lish in a Jeff Gordon hat!

Grand Marshal at a charity golf tournament in Billings, MT
Above: the beautiful Miss Tillie Hoefer (*on the left*) and
Miss Oil Country, K. C. Chatwood (*on the right*)

Putting "Pool Style" with my cane
At a charity golf tournament in San Louis Obispo, CA
(09-06-2013).

After a Live Radio Interview
Above: with super K105FM radio talk show hosts Misty Thomas and Mark Buckles of the live radio show *In the Know,* in Leitchfield, Kentucky (2013).

"Brothers"
My "brother" John Barton, Leitchfield, KY.

with my summer sports clinic team leader
Above: with my incredible Team Leader Kirstin at the
V.A. Summer Sports Clinic in San Diego, CA.
Below: Love it when good friends come for coffee.

Marie Frandsen the most awesome coffee friend ever

The Squire Lounge, Billings, MT
Above: At the Squire Lounge with (L-R) Jim Lish, Jeff Flatness, me, George Blackard, Luke Walker, and Anthony Noe (07-20-2013).

Below: At the Squire, with dear friend JoLynne Flatness (07-20-2013).

Left: Country Singer Nathan Osmond, a good friend and supporter of our military and veterans.

Nathan Osmond, Country Singer

Right: Anthony Swafford, author of the bestselling books *Jarhead* and *Hotels, Hospitals and Jails*. I was honored to learn some valuable things from him and call him my friend.

Anthony Swafford, best-selling author

Below: My "Brother" David Aitken; not just strong, "Jersey Strong!" at San Diego, CA (September 2013).

Below: With friend Cameron Clapp (*left*) and my instructor, mentor, and friend Brad Howe.

Operation Restoration, Pismo Beach, CA (09-08-2013).

Operation Restoration
Above: At Pismo Beach, CA, with friend Chelsea Mae.

My good friend from England
Above: Eddie Platter; Leicester all the way "mate!"

Above: Visiting our wounded soldiers at Ft Knox, KY (2013).

Above: At the Dan G. Dolan Memorial Motorcycle Run, with Gold Star Dad Tim Dolan and Gary Yokum. Men I am honored to be friends with. (08-03-2013)

Above: with Utah VA Volunteer Services Manager and friend, Belinda Karabatsos, always caring for veterans!

Below: My dear, kindhearted friend Rachel Bowman. Don't forget to step on your awesome dad's toe for me (Joe is a giant among men) and give a hug to Mom too.

Below: My buddy Blake headed to Utah
(07-28-2013).

Above: My sisters Carole Duke and April Lish at a Purple
Heart Memorial in Billings, MT (07-24-2013

Blacky. Gordy and Harold

Phil Black *(left)*, me, and Harold on the right . . .
In memory of our dear friend

Harold Fenn

United States Navy Veteran
Honest as the day is long, a patriot, a damn fine man!

March 27, 1926 - September 20, 2013

All Gave Some . . .

G.L. EWELL

Battle Cross

. . . Some Gave All!

. . . Some Are Still Giving!

The End
—